Candid

The Musings of a Prince

"Prince" Letif Belcher

Copyright © 2022 RaShaun L Belcher
All rights reserved.
ISBN: **9798353056638**

DEDICATION

My parents, Brad and Toni Belcher. Thank you for all you've taught me and all you'll continue to teach me!

My siblings, thank you for your support and protection. I hope I'm making you proud.

My chosen family. I'm not naming you all individually, you know who you are. Thank you for keeping me humble and grounded.

Aunt Debbie, this book is only happening because you kept suggesting it! I hope this meets your expectations!

Obsidian Rain, when I told you about the concept of this book, you simply asked, "Well what are you waiting for?" Thank you for lighting the fire.

P. Rose, my collaborator and muse. Not only did you support me throughout this process, but you held me accountable when I let Imposter Syndrome get the best of me. Thank you for being a part of the journey.

Last but not least, Tristan. Son, even though you may never get to read this I pray that you know that everything I do is to make you proud! I know you're in good hands with Grandpa, Auntie Momo, Uncle Jamal, Great Uncle Way-Way and GG Katherine! Your mom and I love and miss you, Batman!

CONTENTS

Acknowledgments

Am I a Poet?
Who Am I
Marriage Material
I Want You
Job Ad
Lovesick
Hanging by a
Thread
2AM Text
The Box
My City
Scared of Us
I'm Not Woke
My Hidden Talent
Copy & Paste
Wash Your Back
Divorcing My Muse
…For Love
What Are You…
Prose
Debt to Sobriety
When I'm Gone

INTRODUCTION

can·did
/ˈkandəd/

1: marked by or showing honesty: frank a candid discussion.
2: relating to photography of people acting naturally without being posed a candid picture.

I wish I could say that I chose the title of this book. But in its own way, *it* found *me*. Over time I've come to learn that "candid" is the best word used to describe my art. Regardless of the medium.

Regarding poetry, the only way I know how to convey a message is to be as truthful as I know how to be. Telling both my story and that of which the world around me has created.

As far as photography goes, I've rarely found much enjoyment in posed images. In fact, I tend to avoid it because of that very fact. Every image has a story of its own and to pose it is to try to control the story instead of allowing the story to just tell itself. REAL life is beautiful, real life can be sad, real life can be joyful and real life can be confusing as hell. I'm just honored that God chose me to be one of the vessels with the ability to capture it.

That said, welcome to Candid: The Musings of a Prince! I hope you enjoy it. My truth, their truth, THE truth.

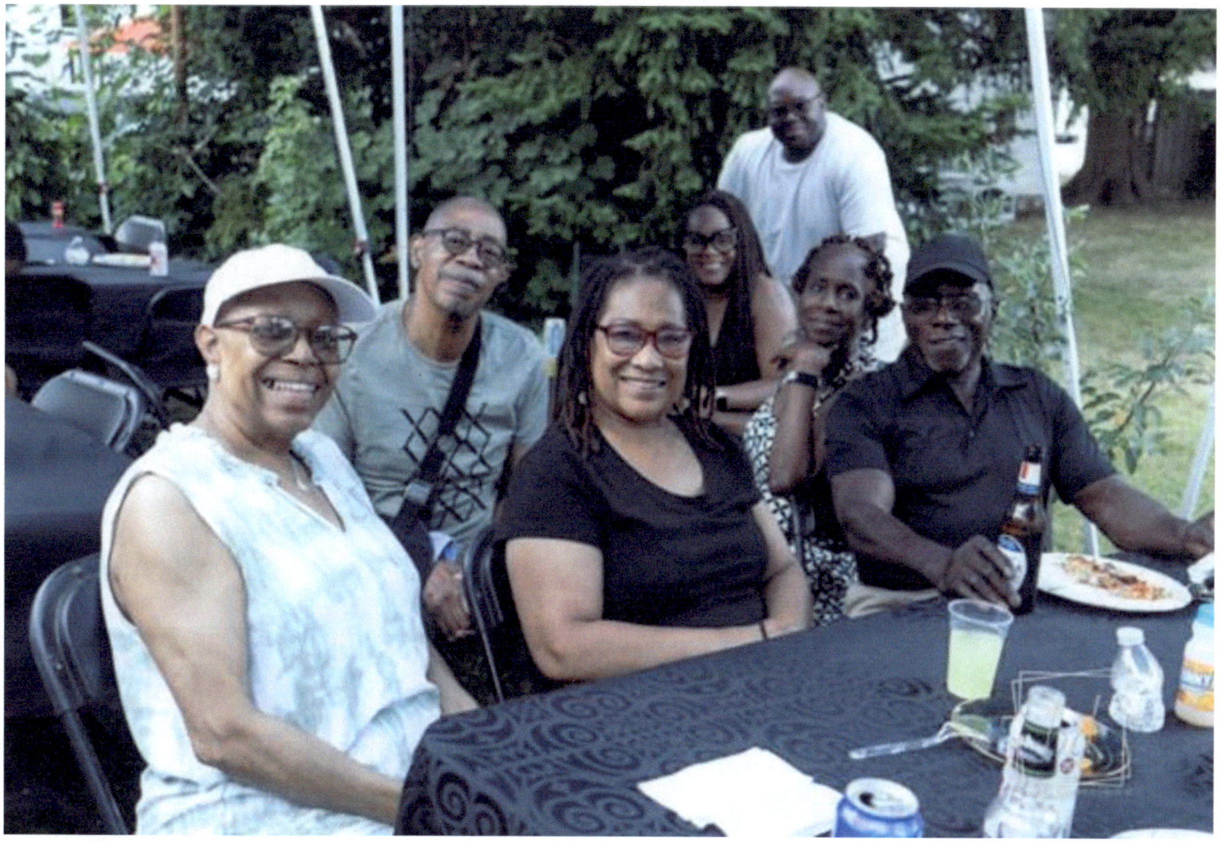

Am I A Poet?

po·et
/ˈpōət/
noun
a person who writes poems.

a person possessing special powers of imagination or expression.

Am I really a poet?

Call it imposter syndrome but I sometimes find myself asking if I'm worthy of the title. Maybe because I don't share the stylistic nature of Poe, Shakespeare, Dubois, Heron or Angelou.

I don't write the pieces that will be studied in creative writing classes or be the scripture around which one molds their world view.

Does it make me less of a poet because I my words don't flow the leaves of sakura in the wind doing the Cherry Blossom Festival?

Can I not call myself a poet because my words don't sound good over a smooth jazz tune

Am I not worthy to pick up a pen because I get eliminated in the 1st round of a slam competition because I require more than 180 seconds to complete a thought?

I'll never be nationally ranked so my name will never ring bells when my face appears on a flier

So perhaps people will not travel across state lines to hear me recite the same 5 poems over the span of that many years

And maybe I'm a fraud because I don't find it that important to memorize or internalize my pieces

Perhaps I can't be a poet because my words don't serve as an aphrodisiac that leads women from the sheets of my journal to the sheets of my bed

Or maybe because I haven't earned the right because I have no desire to push out a poem every day for the month of April because throwing the word "challenge" on something doesn't compel me to do it

I write because I feel, not because I'm told

I write what's on my heart whether or not it fits a rhyme scheme or the words can be acted out theatrically on a stage

I write because it's therapy

I write letters to my present and past selves which is why my art always comes across more conversational than rhythmic

I recite because as alone as I may feel at times, I know that the feeling is all in my mind and maybe my testimony can help others… even if I don't necessarily want them to talk to ME about it

So, am I a poet?

Webster's would affirm that I am

But some of the best novels were just written until the body of work inspired its title.

THE CREATORS' PRAYER

Dear God I come to you as one of your many humble reflections
As you said, we were made in your image and much like you Lord we all exist on this Earth unseen
God, you've created 3 types of people, The Creators, The Consumers and those who hide in between profiting from both sides
And much like you, God, the evidence of everything we create exists all around us while we remain invisible
Staring in the faces of those who choose to remain incredulous to our existence while they benefit daily from the gifts, we bestow upon them
That said, Lord, I pray that you provide a little extra protection to the Creators of the world

I pray that you shine your light on the musicians. The ones that that bring the world joy through chords, whether they be vocal, guitar, violin, piano or power cords and everything in between. Bless the hands of the percussionists who mimic the beat of your heart for the drums in our ears. I pray you protect them from shady record executives and allow their music to be an arrow that pierces through the noise and finds their target audience. Protect them from the janky promoters of venues that profit from the crowds drawn by their name when that pen could have been used to write a check.

I pray that you protect the designers, the true architects of the world. Those with blessed hands that create everything from the clothing on our back to the shoes on our feet, the roofs over our heads and chairs that we seat. The ones that remain unseen unless their names are attached to someone that is simply famous for sharing a bed with one of your reflections. The ones whose names will never be known unless it appears on the front of the tallest building or the moving billboard that we refer to as the front of our shirts. Bless the hands of those that remain nameless as they put their soul into the design of the overpriced sneakers the consumers stand in line for while all the credit goes to the man whose silhouette appears on the sole of our feet.

Please protect the visual artists of the world. The ones whose eyes and hands recreate both the ugliness and beauty of the world you've created. While their messages may not be heard, the melodies that reside in their spirit are conveyed through instruments like, pens, pencils, paint brushes, cameras and electronic styluses. Protect them from the consumers that believe their worth diminishes as soon as their work graces the pixels of their devices. The ones that always have to argue their worth because their gifts can be stolen by a simple screen shot. The very same consumers that don't account for the prices of the pens, paintbrushes, canvases and software that are necessary to create the works that they think they can dictate the prices of but don't think twice about funding a silhouettes 3rd home while they barely have a pot to piss in.

Protect the scribes of the world lord! The ones who write the literature we base our lives and faith upon, the music that shape our personalities and the poetry that paints pictures that we can't create with the tact of the aforementioned visual artists. I pray you bless the hands that write the stories of those you chose not to give their own voices as well as their minds and hearts because no one cares what they're going through as long as they live long enough to share their pain on a page, a microphone or a TV screen for the entertainment of the consumers.

Protect us all from the voices in our own heads that tell us that we can't do the things we know we can. Protect us from the Scylla and Charybdis that make us believe that we're born to be consumers while they consume the fruits from the labor of our creation. Remove us all from the notion that tells us all that we're worth more in death. Because if we don't get our flowers now, we will burn the entire garden and paint the flames.

Amen.

Who Am I

The truth is some mornings I don't even know the answer to this question

I've been many things and I've tried to be many others

I am simultaneously a reflection of God and no one at all

I am the last of 10 children; the one that watched and listened more than I spoke but still never shut up

The one that learned from the mistakes and misfortunes of others but still made many of my own

The one that was more into art than sports but still played every sport I thought would make my father proud of me

I'm the child that would rather be inside with a book or a video game but still played outside because I was always told that having friends would be important some day

Who Am I?

I'm the one who watched what my parents had and fell in love with love at a young age

I held on to some of those good moments and filtered out the bad until I found myself always looking for the Toni to my Brad.

I went from being a serial monogamist to a borderline sex addict until ultimately giving up

Gave up because although I may have cheated once, I was cheated on many times because "Though I'm a great guy, I just lack excitement."

I'm the one that has made every mistake you can make in a relationship but my advice is useless because I'm not attached to someone

Who Am I?

A statistic.

The 1 in every 6 young boys whose 1st sexual encounter was with that of an older woman

Coerced by my childhood babysitter to touch parts of her body that I did not know weren't appropriate until my adolescence

I'm the boy that said nothing to anyone about this until I wrote about it in this piece

So, when people blame victims for taking too long to speak out about their pain, I simply look them in the eye and say #MeToo

Who am I?

I'm a creator

Once a dancer until break dancing broke ME

I also rapped for 5 minutes but ultimately gave up because 3 Stacks said it best, "I'm not a hood nigga, just a nigga from the hood."

Rapping evolved into poetry, I wrote often but never memorized anything and eventually stopped once I let my boys convince me that vulnerability was "for bitches"

So, from that point on I only wrote pro-Black, revolutionary poems to spit at open mic nights

Who am I?
I am who some refer to as a pseudo-revolutionary
Because I don't take selfies with those who may be experiencing the worst phase of their lives

My contributions to society can't be found on Google or social networks

Nor do I care to talk about the work I've done for the applause or accolades

Not in my lifetime will I ever receive award for my deeds and I don't intend to

I just use the privilege I've been blessed with to help others in need because no one deserves to feel like they're alone on a planet inhabited by billions

Most of the good I've done in the last 18 years has been about my journey to be more Christ-like than Christian

Who am I?

A man that lived too much of his life looking for the acceptance of others because it took too long for me to accept myself

I'm a man who didn't know true happiness until I learned to just be me, unapologetically

MARRIAGE MATERIAL
COWRITTEN BY P. ROSE

I'm definitely husband material
but do you have the right needle to thread me into the fabric of your life?
I'm noticing dark shades in the textile that you call your future that make this all feel sketchy.
I wanted to leave but you begged and pleated that I stay.
So maybe if you could trace this out for me, I wouldn't falter to halt-er and comprehend.
Because when my arms drape your bodice, it feels sew amazing and makes our fit seem shearly perfect.
But we need to cut away all our tattered edges and loose ends before we march down the runway to complete our matrimonial composition.

Yes, I am biased…
I am, wife material.
Tailor made for true love.

I have gathered myself together.
Handled the raw edges
Doing the work to better myself…

For me.
For you.
For us.

I have hemmed and pressed my past.
Interfaced with my present self and
I have pinned my future.

A true silhouette of happily ever after.
Altered by our terms.
Our style.

8

I Want you

I want you

In every sense of the phrase

I want you

The first sight I see to begin my days

I want you

to tell me I'm your hearts only desire

I want you

To pour your love all over me, and douse this lonely fire

I want you

To remind me what it feels like to be loved

I want you

To be the reason I forget what loneliness ever was

I want you

To fall asleep every night with your head on my chest

I want you

To dream of one day wearing that white dress

I want you

To be my future and forget our past

I want you
To know that although you weren't my first you will be my last

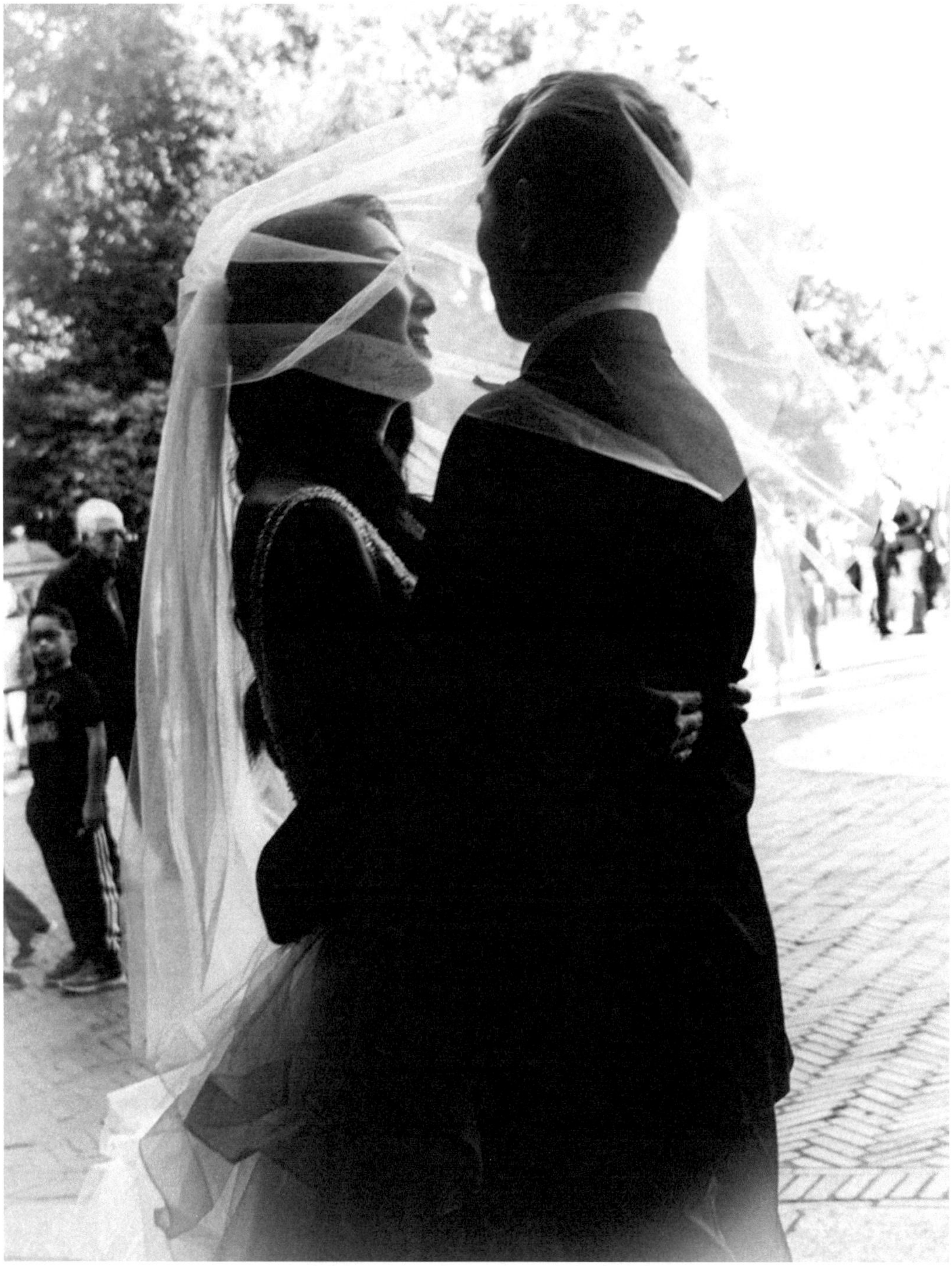

Job Ad

Position: Full-Time Life Partner

Requirements: Must have long-term plans to stay with the company. Must be a very dedicated associate and know how to properly balance business and personal lives. Must be loyal, we're confident that we'll be able to compensate you well enough for your work that seeking a second job wouldn't ever be needed. Plans to grow with the company are greatly appreciated and we'll always keep the possibility in mind. Must be able to hold intelligent conversations and possess a sense of humor. Must be able to handle vigorous physical labor and occasionally work overnight shifts. Good communication skills are also a must.

Job Description: Full-Time companion, will work very closely with the owner of the company as well as associates and occasional visits to parent companies. Will provide emotional, mental, spiritual, and moral support.

R.L. Belcher and Associates appreciates you for reading this Job Ad but we only encourage serious applicants. Part-time applicants need not apply.

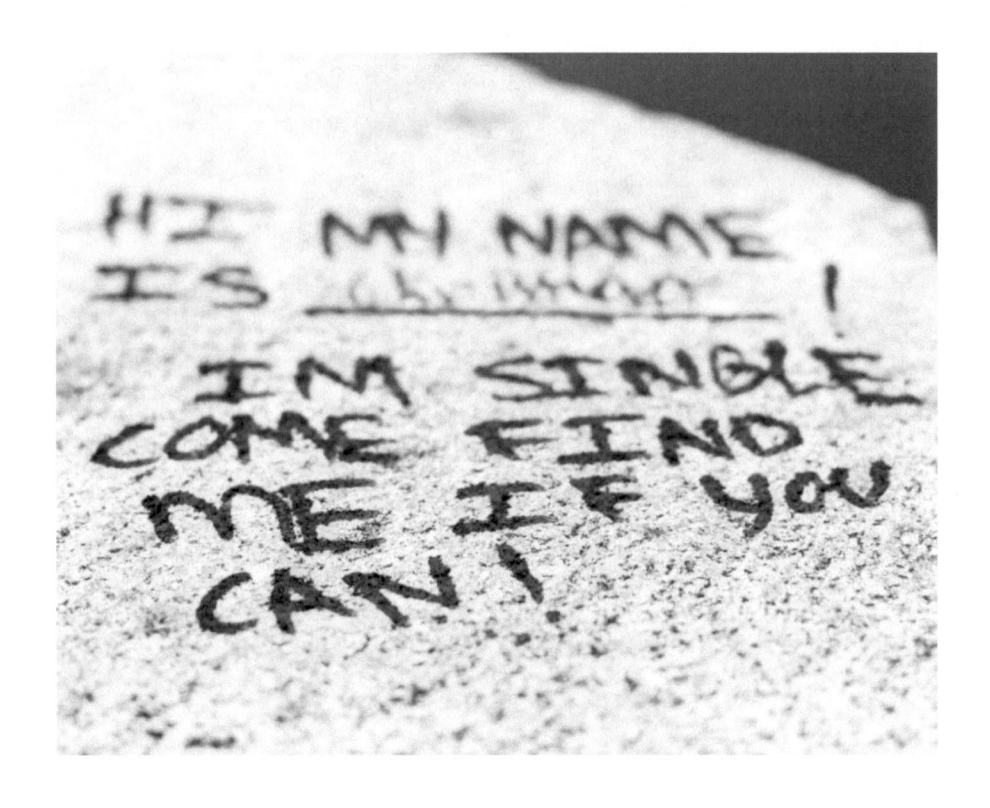

LOVESICK
(072207)

I never been the type of dude to feel regret
I know I've done things you're never gonna forget
I cheated
I mean I only skimmed through love's manual, I skipped a few steps
Defeated
and I'm a bad sport
I was never too good at catch up
ur presence missed it hits like a chev' truck
with the HEMI in it
hit the bottom of many bottles
surpassed the Henny limit
like a lost soul
holdin on the false hope
that you would come back to me any minute
these tears?
I've cried rivers that lead to oceans on my pillow
My fear?
Karma's already came in full circle and I'm still weeping like a willow.
It's clear
I'm dead in your eyes, but you refuse to be a widow
I'm here
You say you don't hate me; I KNOW you don't love me your heart is somewhere in the middle
I'm vexxed
I know you've moved on; I saw u 2 together
Now I'm a mess
I must seem desperate the more u read this letter
I had to get it off my chest
should u come back, it's promised to get better
we've yet to reach our apex

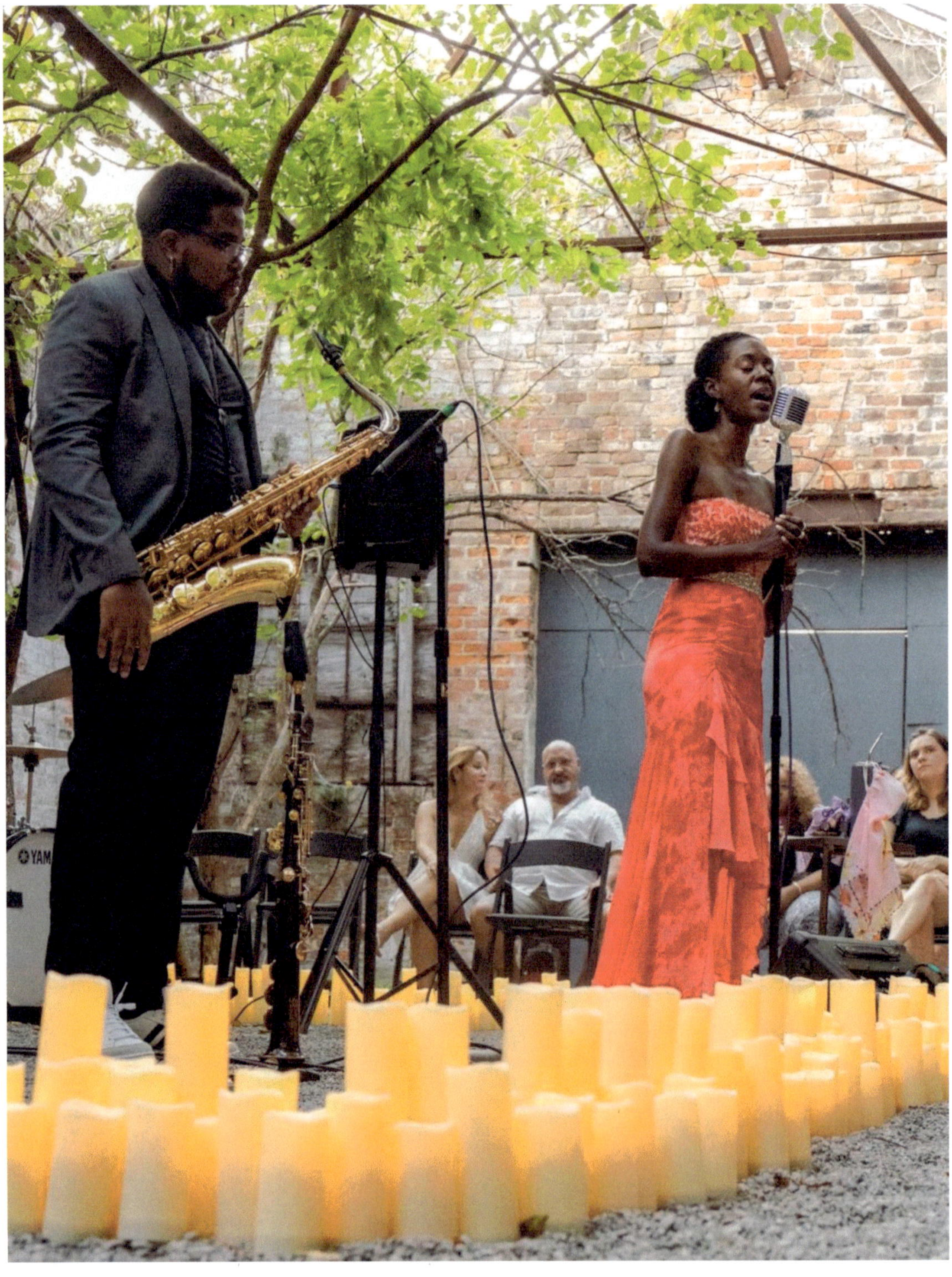

Hanging by a Thread

I'm a 10-year-old Camel colored Banana Republic trench coat.
To passers-by I LOOK perfect. Great looking, classy and they all think they want me; or something like me.
But there's one major flaw.... that button hanging on for dear life on that frayed thread.
As with every coat there's a decision... to sew the button back on or cut it off as if it never belonged.
I tend to think I look amazing with this button. I feel that it complements me and frankly I don't want to imagine myself without it.
This frayed thread is like a memory of all we've been through.
The violent storms and calm breezes
the ugly stains and the many trips to the cleaners to make it look brand new
and even the random people to borrow it from time to time
Some would say the thread is frayed for a reason
not even to bother sewing it back on
just get a new button and sew it on with new thread
but I don't think anyone realizes how hard it is to find another button that can match the one that I have currently hanging on
It'll be like searching a needle in a haystack to find a button exactly like or better than the one I had
and for all that I'd rather just go without one
just forget the button was ever there and make what was incomplete seem like it was a choice to remove
or even better... that it was never there to begin with.
That decision is still one that remains.
For now, I'm just going to let this button hang right where it is until I decide...
or until it's just disappears. As buttons seem to do.

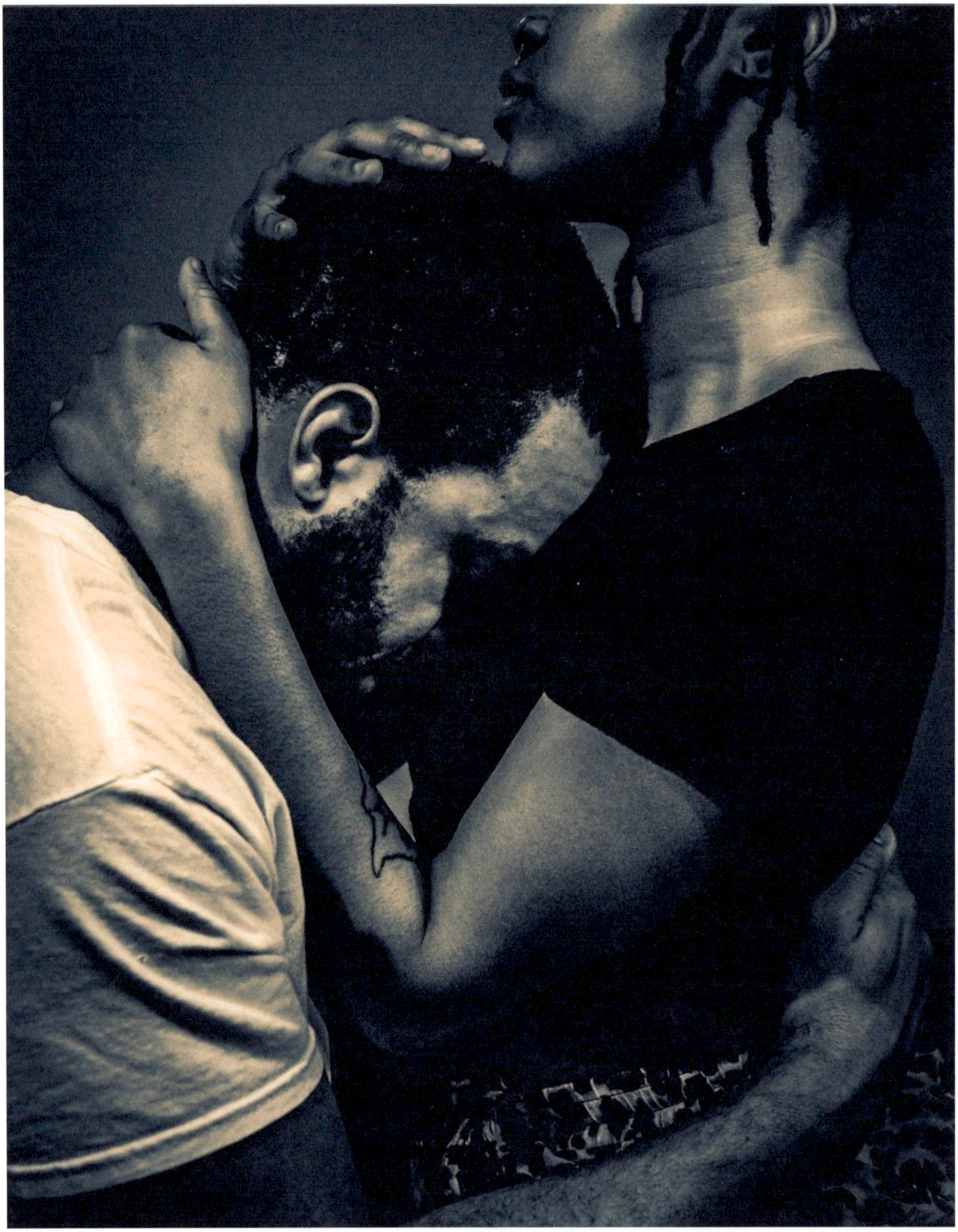

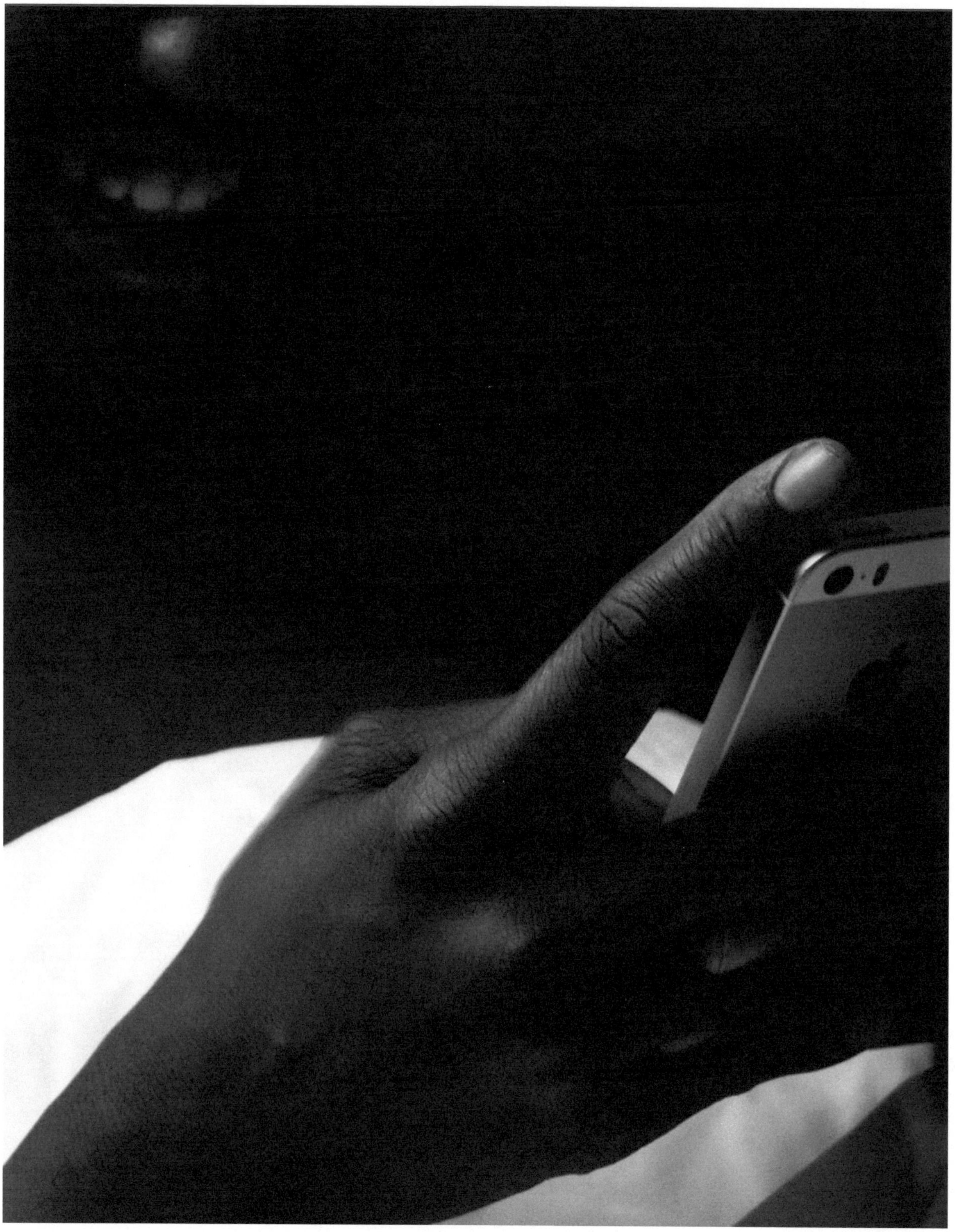

2AM Text

You just run across my mind
You just run across my mind
You just run across my mind
You just run across my mind

Hey bighead
Listen, I wish I could say I'm sorry about this hour

But if we're being honest, I wanted to shoot a quick shot

See, I was just watching Martin and an Applebee's commercial came on

And I got flashbacks of the night we went there for dinner and saw that hotel outside the window

And we decided to skip dinner and head straight to dessert

You treated me like ice cream and you were my molten lava cake

I still remember the way you giggled when you saw the way your caramel dripped my goatee

So enthralled by the way the moon illuminated your face while you slept

I would stay up and find the constellations in your freckles

I still remember the lil games you'd play like teasing me public, getting me aroused

and walking away because you wanted me to punish you for it whenever we made it home

You liked to do things like that, things like losing your keys so you'd have an excuse to stay the night

Or puttin on my favorite dress when you went out with your girls
cuz you knew as soon as you'd post a selfie that I was gonna hop in your DM's and it worked EVERY time

You used to call me your favorite 2am text

Cuz you knew I hated the club life so you knew where I'd be when you got out

But there was that one time...
We happened to be in the same bar on the same night

I'd watch while other men bought you drinks

Until you shot me a look that gave me the fearless confidence to walk over and kiss you

I don't know what came over me when I threw a $20 on the counter and tell that poor man, "Thanks, we'll take care of the tip"

So turned on by this you couldn't even wait till we got home

We pulled over in a church parking lot and you called out to God while I spoke in tongues

I still remember that Cheshire cat grin you'd have when you reached your climax

That smile...

The 2nd most beautiful curve on your body only behind that deep ass arch in your back

An arch so deep that when you slept, the small of your back never touched the bed

Unless your legs were on my shoulders as they often tended to be

It always worked because we never wanted commitment

Most times we literally just came and went

Till one day you got a man and I got in my feelings

I stopped hittin you up outta respect until you sent me nudes asking if I thought he'd like them

Thought even that was your way of saying good bye...

Then you showed up to my house on Valentine's Day in the lingerie he bought you cuz he went away to all-star weekend

I wasn't mad either cuz just like I was your favorite 2am text, you were my favorite notification

We were no good for one another but we were even worse to others because of each other

It's TRUE that good sex is like a drug cuz you're no good for me but you just make me feel so good

And I saw you like mufasa's post about how good toxic sex is

So, what's up? It's like quarter to 2 and if you're in the bar I hope you read this before you head home.

The key is in the usual spot. I'll see you soon

THE BOX

Every time I get up an open mic, I'm reminded of the time I was at an event that

I was hired to photograph and when I asked to be placed on the list, I was met with the reply,

"Well, if you're on the mic, then who's going to take the pictures?"

As if somehow the 1/200th of a second that it takes me to snap a photo is more

important to you than the 3 minutes it takes me to stand up here and speak my mind.

But to your point, I may have missed a few good shots because I was in the back of the room during the event revising this piece

But I digress

it took me that same 200th of a second to realize that my peers have put me into a box

Think about that for a minute... what does that phrase mean?

Dictionary.com refers to a box as a receptacle you put a gift in for safe keeping.

Understanding that my mind is the gift I wonder who or what exactly we're to trying to keep safe?

Do my hands forget how to write when I lift a camera?

Do you forget how to speak when you sing?

Do your feet forget how to walk when you dance?

Telling an artist that they can't exhibit more than one gift is like telling the sun that it can't be bright and warm at the same time.

Trying to limit a true creative to 1 gift is like telling a flower that it can't be beautiful and vibrant or

like telling a woman she can't be both attractive and intelligent.

It sounds like bullshit when you put it that way, right?

So, what are we keeping safe?

Imagine if Quincy Jones had told Will Smith he'd never be more than a rapper

Imagine if Jill Scott had stuck to poetry and never tried to sing a note

Or if Ava Duvernay stuck to journalism and didn't pick up her 1st camera at the age of 32

Or if anyone told Beyoncé that she can't act-uallyyyyyy

She may wanna stick to music

But imagine how I feel when I tell you I wanna compete in your next slam

And rather than give me a verbal answer
You show me through your actions

You showed me when you posted the flyer of your chosen poets and my face isn't on it!

In fact, you turned up the volume on this message when the faces on the flyer were all a collage of the faces that I've shot
I heard you

Though I heard you, the message was unclear
I don't know if you were trying to me, I was whack or just not yet ready

Or maybe you just wanted me to think that because you knew it would light a fire under my ass so I would practice spitting the piece the way i am right now.
But trust me, I heard you

Maybe your message was that you think I lack the ability to impress the judges

You've forgotten one thing; I don't write what I write for acceptance and slam scores

But I hear you

Maybe the message was that you don't think I have the ability to engage with an audience

As if I can't engage all 5 senses

As if you don't see me before you pouring out my heart

As if you can't taste the passion that I exude while on a stage

Or smell the fear and anxiety I had to overcome in order to recite this

Or feel the anger in my voice for needing to write this in the 1st place

Can you hear me

I've heard you!

I think I figured out something else too

The only thing my "haters" are trying to protect is their fragile sense of security

The so- called "creatives" that have never challenged themselves farther than that one thing they were told they do well.

Or, worse, the narcissists that feel that because they failed, you could never surpass them.

This box that you've built for me feels more like a casket but i will not lay down in it to make you feel comfortable

and you will not bury my gift

Imagine, trying to take a step out of your own box because you are not one-dimensional

Cuz I know myself and I can walk into any event and be the photographer, the host, the dj and the feature.

And know this

I'm not just your photographer

I'm not your DJ

I'm not your poet

Erykah Badu said "We were made in his image so call us by our names"

So, from this point forward you will only address me as The Creator

And though I may occasionally share my gifts with you, understand that however the universe

decides through speak to me at any given moment was never intended for your consumption

So, if this piece resonates with you, don't allow the words of others limit your creativity

If you wake up tomorrow morning with something on your heart, do it

May the universe be with you and may this piece be your box cutter

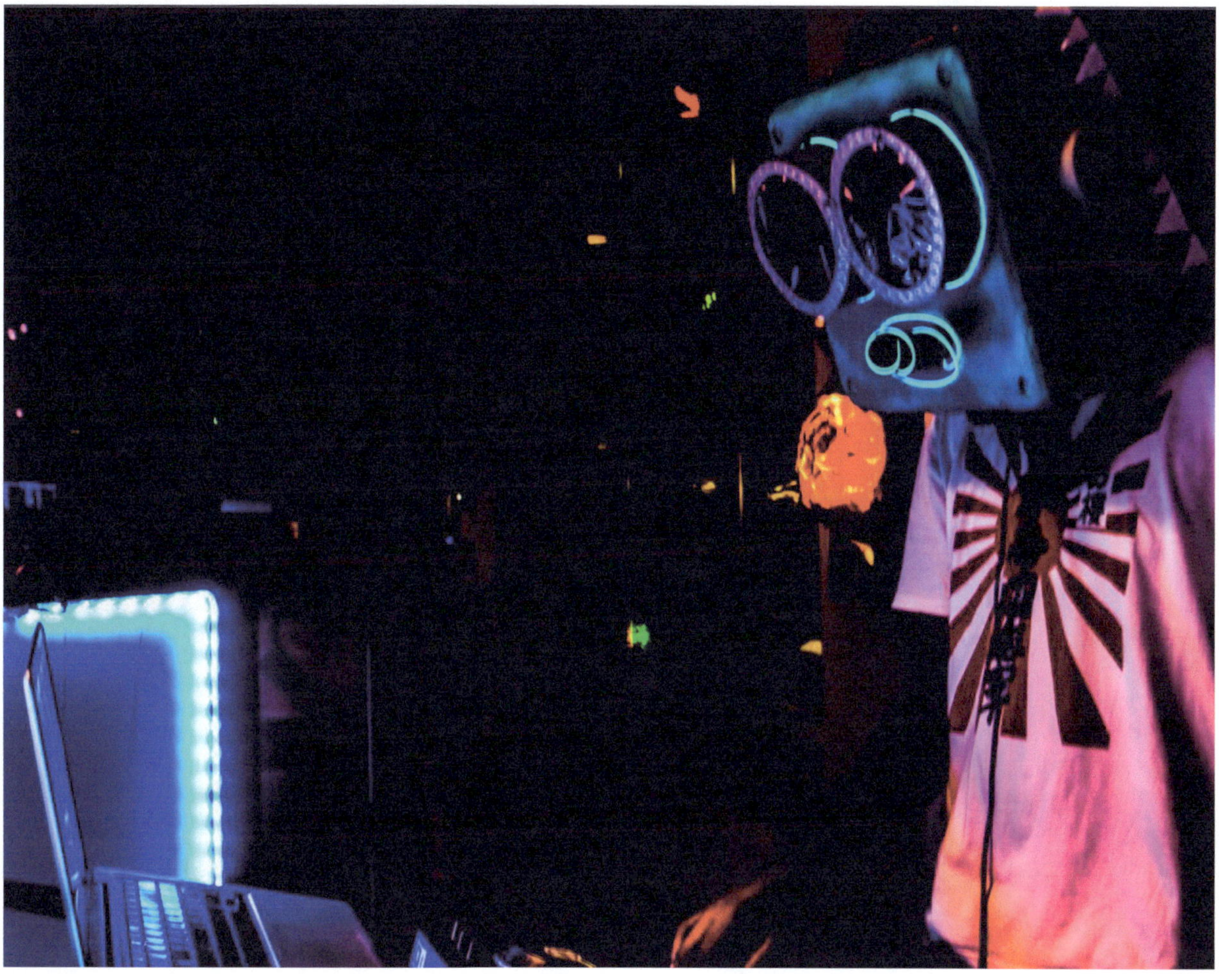

MY CITY

I can remember the 1st time I attempted to hang out with some kids from outside my community.

My best friend's dad moved to Shelton and registered him into Shelton High because he didn't want him coming up through the Bridgeport School system

I had gone to one of his basketball games. And met his new white friends who thought I was pretty cool until he referred to me as his friend from Bridgeport

It was at this very moment that you could immediately see the horror on their faces as they each took a step back.

I was only 14 but even then, I could tell that because of my address they immediately thought less of me

And that step back was as if they thought that the poverty, they assumed I lived in was contagious.

20 years later, you can look out your window and see those very same people walking their dogs after midnight

Those same young girls are now grown women that hang out in bars around town because they love the adventure of flirting with black men

Check this out

My block is not your field trip

My stoop is not your petting zoo

And my lifestyle is not your FUCKIN punchline

You come to our spaces to tell jokes about how you come to our neighborhoods because the food is better

Imagine how good the food would be in yours had your ancestors actually taken the time to learn to use the seasoning they colonized the world to steal

Which is why I can only laugh when my people invite you to their imaginary cookouts

Because they were easily amused by your mediocre appropriation of our culture

You ask why we celebrate black history

It's because if you don't learn from life's lessons, then you're doomed to repeat em

Example: in 1492, white folks travel the new world where indigenous people taught them how to grow crops and feed themselves
Only to be repaid with smallpox blankets and genocide

Nearly 200 Years later, they travel to Africa and enslave its people and bring them here to build this country

400 years later the descendants of those white folks travel to the neighborhoods they forced us in, we teach them fashion and culture only to be repaid with the crack epidemic and mass incarceration

So, while You laugh about our history of crack addiction and go home to your cozy home

Understand that when we went home, we had to wipe our feet before we walked in the house.

Not because of bringing dirt in the house but because when looked at my soles Air Jordan was dunkin' blue tops

For those that don't understand that it meant we wiped crack vials out the treads of our sneakers

So, if I had to explain that to you, I know you could never walk in my shoes

And please spare me your "but that's not me" speech

Because we all know the white man is the master of the rebrand.

From slavery to incarceration

From colonizer to gentrification

From white supremacist to republican

From republican to alt right

And my favorite from all lives matter to "ally"

And more recently, from red lining to luxury apartments

Trust and believe, we know what's happening when you build a Bass Pro Shop in a city where the people don't fish

And require a 700-credit score to live in a city where the average score is around 6

The only thing I find funny is that, in this city

When a black man commits a felony in this city, he eventually becomes an ex-con

When a white man commits a felony in this city, he eventually becomes the mayor

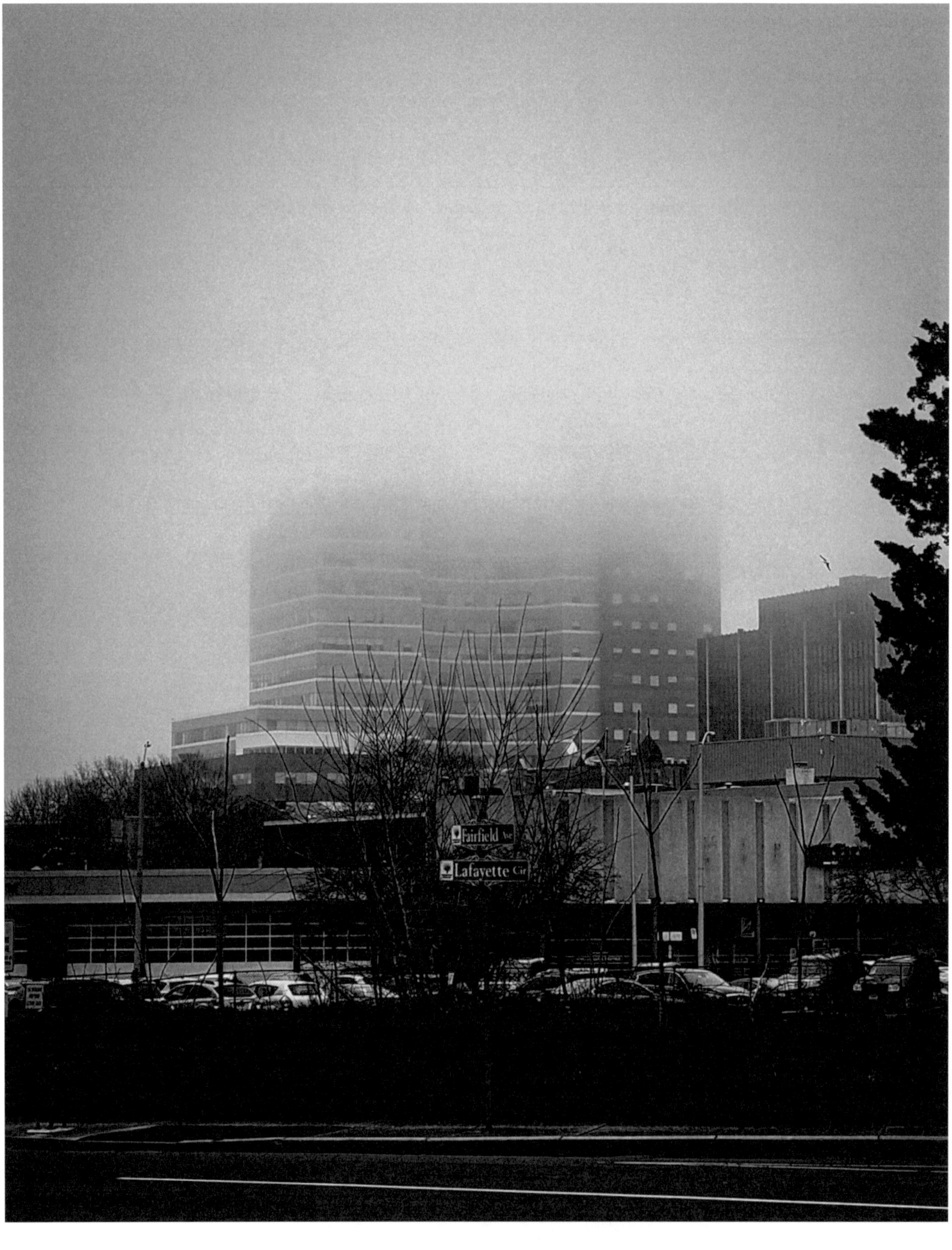
Fairfield Ave
Lafayette Cir

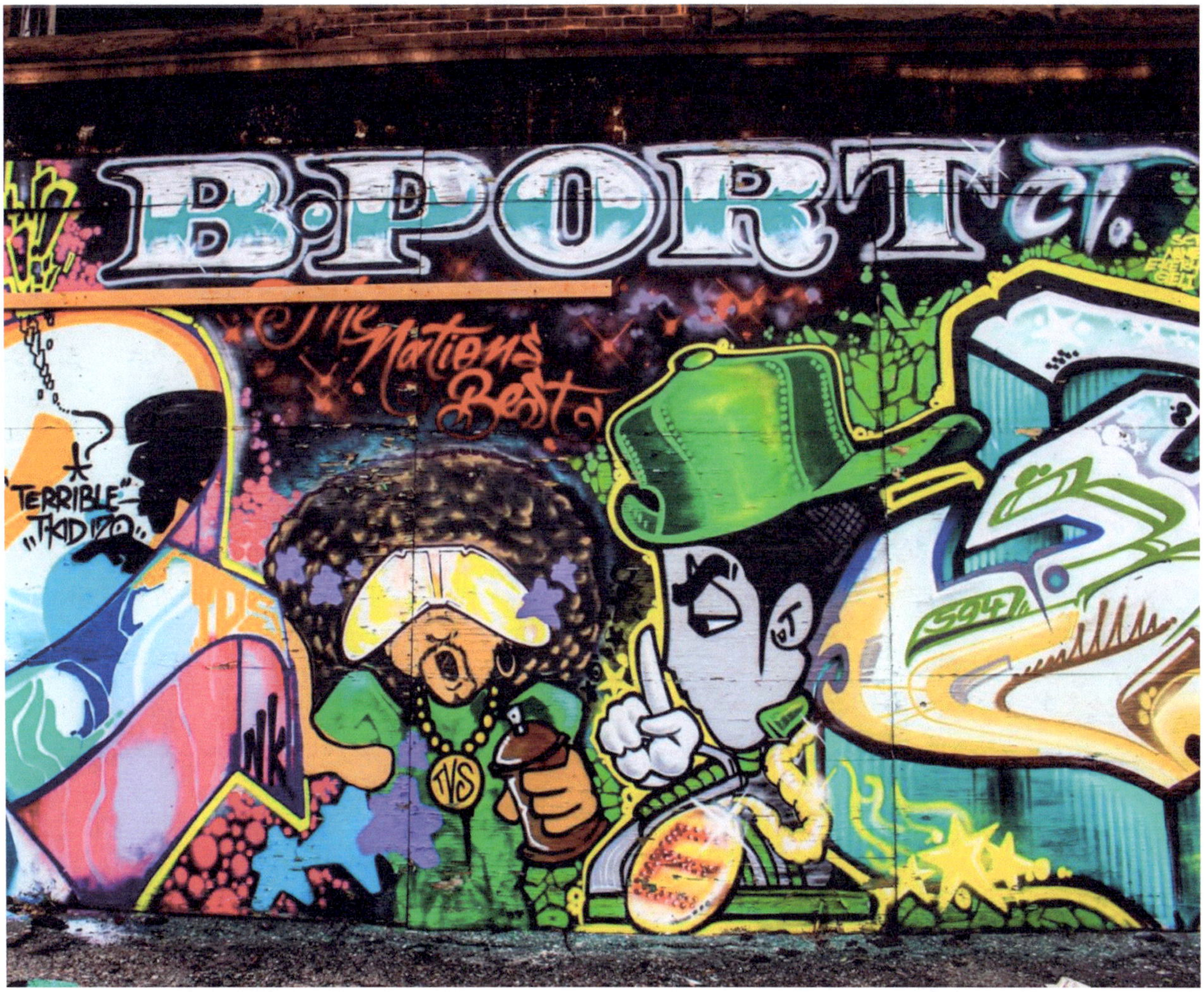
B.PORT CT.
The Nations Best
"TERRIBLE"
TVS

SCARED OF US

I think they scared of us

I mean... this isn't a baseless accusation, right?

I mean they built a system where our schools and hospitals are underfunded and our people live in subhuman conditions

It took 6 years for Flint, MI to get water clean enough to bathe in but over in the Ozarks white folks break quarantine to party in it.

I think they scared of us because our most gifted children are diagnosed with ADHD

And drugged so they become mental zombies and never reach their full potential while c and d grade average white folks run the country

I think they're scared of us

Because we have to teach our children to make you comfortable because at any given moment, we're 4 keystrokes away from our execution

9-1-1-sends us back to the heavens from which we've ascended

Because you're offended that we use a 5-letter word to describe you but you've used one to describe us since we've been here

What's that? Oh, 'cuz I thought a member of the Keyboard Karen Klan said somethin'

See I know you scared of us!

'Cuz every time you send your people to start a riot during our protest you misquote Martin Luther King the same way you do the Bible

But leave out the part where you killed him because he changed his mind

Then gave us a holiday to celebrate him the way you want him to be remembered

like an abusive parent giving their child a new toy after a beating

I think they scared of us! Cuz look at how quick these big corporations are to put black Lives Matter on their websites

Because they're more aware of our buying power than we are and its sad to say that they also know my people are gullible enough to say "well they said it on Twitter so it must be true right?

How come no one talks about the way you disrespect my flag by making red blood pour from a black body onto God's green earth
While you kneel on the back of our necks

So, I'm not too concerned about your red, white and blue 'cuz I'll bet my freedom papers you don't even know what the colors stand for

Which is why you fall for anything your president tells you

And y'all knew damn well that Kaep wasn't kneeling about a damn flag

You just conjured up a false narrative to create a diversion

I know we're both playing this same media game

But it's hard because I hold the controller while you are the controller

So, we apologize to our ancestors for the sacrifices they made

but we gotta tear this system apart cuz the fuckin game cheatin

Why? 'Cuz I think they scared of us!

I'M NOT WOKE

I am not woke.
But I am the son of a Black Panther

So, much like Starr in The Hate U Give
My father made me study the 10-step program
Before I could play outside

In fact, The Miseducation of The Negro, The Autobiography of Malcolm X, and Bobby Seale's Seize the Time were all required reading in my household before I even started my 1st day of high school

And you know what the moral of the story is? I've already forgotten more than some of you so-called woke niggas will ever know

And I've also done the math: See I'm 3 years older than Colin Kaepernick

Which means he was still throwin footballs around the backyard

When my dad took me to my 1st football game, saw me stand for the national anthem and said,

"Sit yo butt down that anthem ain't for you"

And when my homeroom teacher assaulted me for refusing to stand for the anthem
There was no social media for everyone to pretend they cared for a day

See I, Too, have had NYPD's gun in my face
when I was 22

But I can only guess the universe kept me alive because hashtags were still pound signs

So, if I died that night, I don't think the world would have known that my Black Life Mattered yet

You see I'm not woke but I'm conscious enough to know that there's a handful of words that could draw a reaction from the audience at any open mic night

chakras

manifest

Queen

Entrepreneur

And while we on the subject of entrepreneurs

I'm tired of yall negros calling me a slave cuz I get up to go work for "mas'sa" 4 days a week.

Cuz last time I checked, my slave wages paid for all tee shirts, books and mixtapes yall niggas keep tryna sell me

My slave wages paid for the gas to drive you to spend your last $20 on weed

and even paid for you to sit in these open mics and tell me how much better than me you are

cuz you just quit your 3rd job this year because you have "Authority Issues"

But we ain't gonna talk about that tonight

I am not woke!

But I have to laugh at the audacity of you to think I care about your opinions on my diet
On your tight ass Prince Akeem diet cuz you only eat consume the freshest juices and berries

And giving me some unsolicited speech because I enjoy a cheeseburger after a night at the bar while you smoke your cigarette

Talking to me about you only eat organic
When all organic means is that it's treated with government approved chemicals

Explaining to me that my late eating habits are the reason I'm overweight while you herald yourself as the portrait of black fitness
Hotep hooray for you, my nigga!

'Cuz whether this wing comes a chicken or a cauliflower you still can't square up with me physically or mentally

no estoy despierto

At least those were her words when she called me a disgrace to "good black men" because the mother of my 1st child is Puerto Rican

The truth is, whether it be 3A or 4C, I just happen to have a weakness for curly hair

And I've seen what her grandfather looked like.

That man's skin was darker than mine; which told me that the biggest difference between her lineage and mine was the distance between the 2 points where the slave ship docked.

And if you truly knew the history of American Law you would know that the "One drop rule" dictates I could impregnate any woman of any race but because of my DNA whether my son was white, red or blue, THEY would only see a BLACK man.

I'm not woke

but my eyes are open wide enough to see that you're bout to sit me down and ask me to join another half-assed community activist group

I'm done watching so called "leaders" stand in front of a room and tell me about the finish line

they're fantasizing about and expect ME to map out their path from point A to point B and only to take the credit and smile for News 12

Nothing about me desires to align myself with a bunch'a "bout 2" niggas

For those that don't know, a "bout 2" nigga is someone that always going on and on about some shit they "Bout 2" do but never actually does.

You think wokeness is your ally. I was born into the revolution, molded by it. I didn't see "Consciousness" till I was already a man but by then it was blinding

And for you "wokies" that don't like this piece, let me end this with a quote

"I'm blacker than the ace of spades and more militant than you and your whole damned army put together.

And while you're out there chanting at rallies and brow beating politicians, I'm taking out any money frontin' sucker on a humble that gets in my way, so I'll tell you what.

When your so-called Revolution starts, you call me and I'll be right down in front showing you how it's done.

But until then, you need to SHUT THE FUCK UP when grown folks is talkin!"

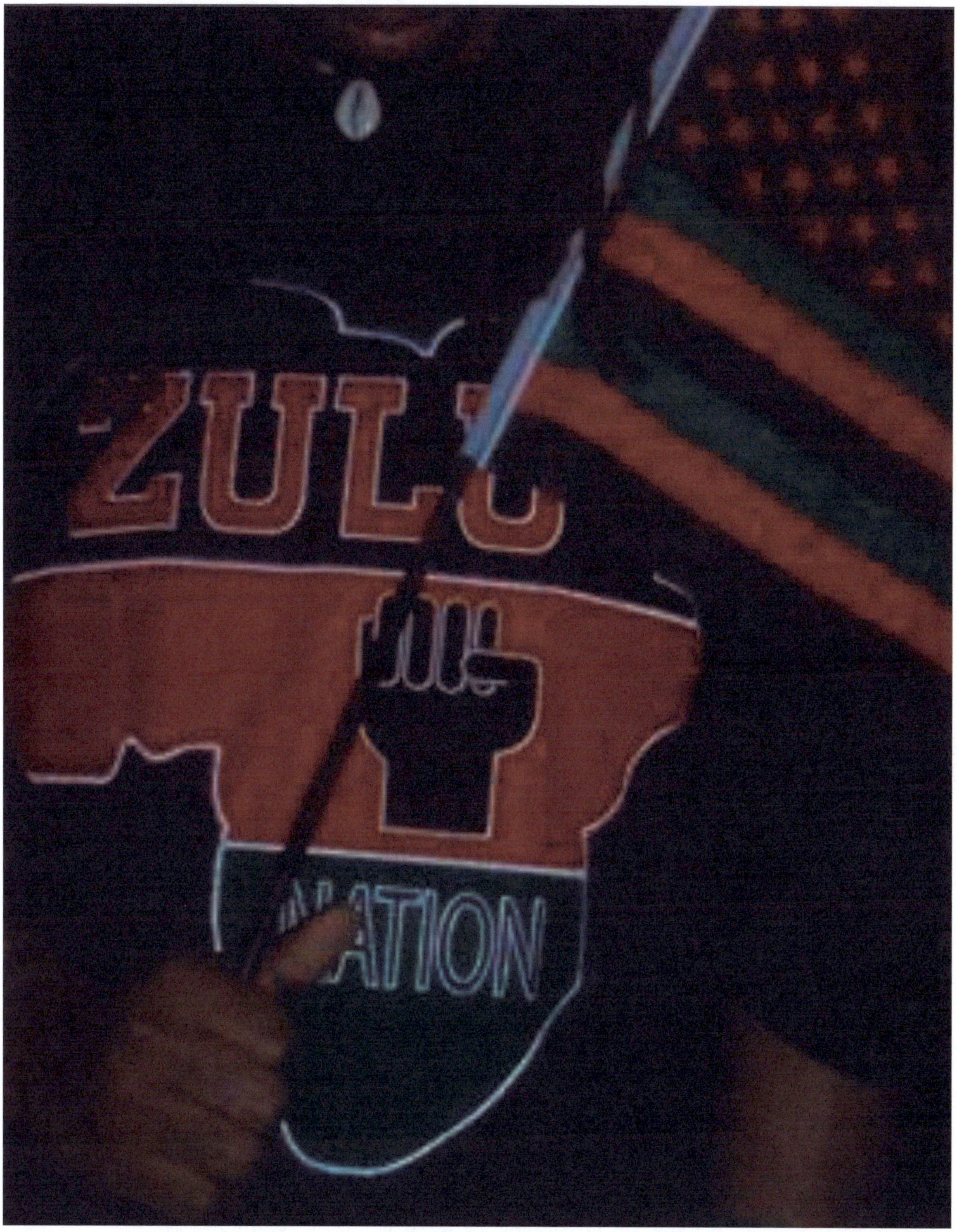

My Hidden Talent

There used to be a time in interviews back in the day when they would ask a person, "What hidden talent do you have?"

I rarely ever listened to the answer because I would always sit and wonder what mine is

ACHIEVEMENT UNLOCKED!

After 36 years on this earth, I've found a talent so hidden that when I was doing it, I never knew that I was

A skill I've honed to such a point that its second nature

Something that comes to me as easily as breathing

And do you know what that is?

It's something that's best summed up in 2 simple words:

EMOTIONAL DETACHMENT

Disappointed?

Is it because I got your Hopes up anticipating something great

only to deflate those feelings with the truth like dropping a brick on a balloon?

Because that's what love feels like

Unless the balloon somehow rolls out of the way before the brick falls so it misses the painful end of the brick's journey back to earth

I can't believe I missed it, though

I've been surrounded by the evidence my entire life

The huge list of unfinished books, video games and tv series' that I loved so much and walked away from so I couldn't be disappointed by the way it ended

How many funerals did I sit through tear-free because once I realized the person was on their way out, I distanced myself so it wouldn't hurt when the inevitable occurred?

my sister's cancer came back stronger than it did the 1st time and I couldn't even bring myself to visit her or see if she needed anything

My grandmother passed away and I showed up to Poetz Realm like nothing had ever happened

Someone even went as far as complimenting my strength because I made it through my father's funeral without shedding a single tear

I stood in silence because this was like that epic moment that I realized that what I was exhibiting was actually the opposite of strength

What I'm showing is weakness

My grip on life is so weak that when it moves too fast, I simply let go and let it move forward without me

A weakness that left the hospital when my father was on his deathbed and woke up the next morning with a hangover to voicemails that he passed

So weak that as I write this, I've I mentally and emotionally left my relationship 4 months ago

I just haven't told *her* yet

Do you know what that feels like?

As if I didn't already prove my point, I emotionally detached myself from this piece and stopped writing it

COPY & PASTE

I'm sick of this! When is the cycle of violence going to end?! Another Black body, another Black life taken too soon by those sworn to protect them! Another ~~overseer~~ officer that decided in the moment to also assume the role of judge, jury and executioner. Another unarmed Black person that won't be making it home for dinner with their family. I fear for my children! I fear for myself! How long until it's one of my loved ones' names behind a hashtag? We have to boycott! We have to make them hear our voices! Meet me down at [redacted] and we'll march to the police station until they hear us! #SayTheirNames #BlackLivesMatter

[COPY]

[redacted] was riding his bicycle through the hushed streets of [redacted]., one evening when a police officer noticed that the bike had no lights and that he was weaving in and out of traffic. [redacted] stopped and the pair exchanged words until [redacted] fled, ditching the bicycle. The officer caught up and a struggle ensued. 7 shots later, [redacted] laid dead in the bushes near an apartment complex.

[PASTE]

[redacted] a 12-year-old boy was slain in [redacted] by a police officer after police responded to a dispatch regarding a male with a gun. The caller reported that a male was pointing a pistol at random people. "I knew it was a gun and I knew it was coming out" said the officer who shot [redacted] twice in the torso. [redacted] died in the hospital the next day.

[RIGHT-CLICK; PASTE]

[redacted] was murdered was murdered by a white police officer while being arrested for the suspicion of using a counterfeit $20 bill. [redacted] had shown signs of anxiety; stating that he had feelings of claustrophobia and difficulty breathing. After several minutes with a knee on his neck, [redacted] stopped talking as bystanders pleaded the officer to lift his knee from [redacted] neck. Autopsy reports ruled the death to be a homicide.

[TEARFULLY, PASTE]

28-year-old [redacted] was found hanged in a jail cell after being arrested during a traffic stop. Her arrest was partially recorded by a bystander's cell phone as well as her own. In the bystander's video [redacted] is seen lying prone on the ground stating that she cannot hear after her head was slammed into the ground to which the officer responded, "Good'. Her death was initially ruled a suicide as reports say she used a garbage bag to hang herself despite abrasions on her hands and wrists.

[CTRL+V]

[redacted] was fatally shot in her bed as 7 police officers forced entry into her apartment in pursuit of her ex-boyfriend. According to her boyfriend, he fired a shot out of fear, believing that it was her ex-boyfriend returning to her apartment as the officers did not announce themselves. He fired hit one of the officers in the leg. Officers then returned fire and shot [redacted] 5 times.

[RIGHT CLICK, PAUSE, PASTE]

[redacted] was murdered at close range during a traffic stop after informing an officer that he had a registered firearm in the vehicle. Upon being informed, the officer then responded, "Don't reach for it then." There was a back-and-forth exchange while [redacted] assumedly searched for the car's registration as the officer thought he was reaching for the firearm, he discharged 5 shots into [redacted] in front of his girlfriend and, then, 4-year-old child.

[SHUT DOWN]

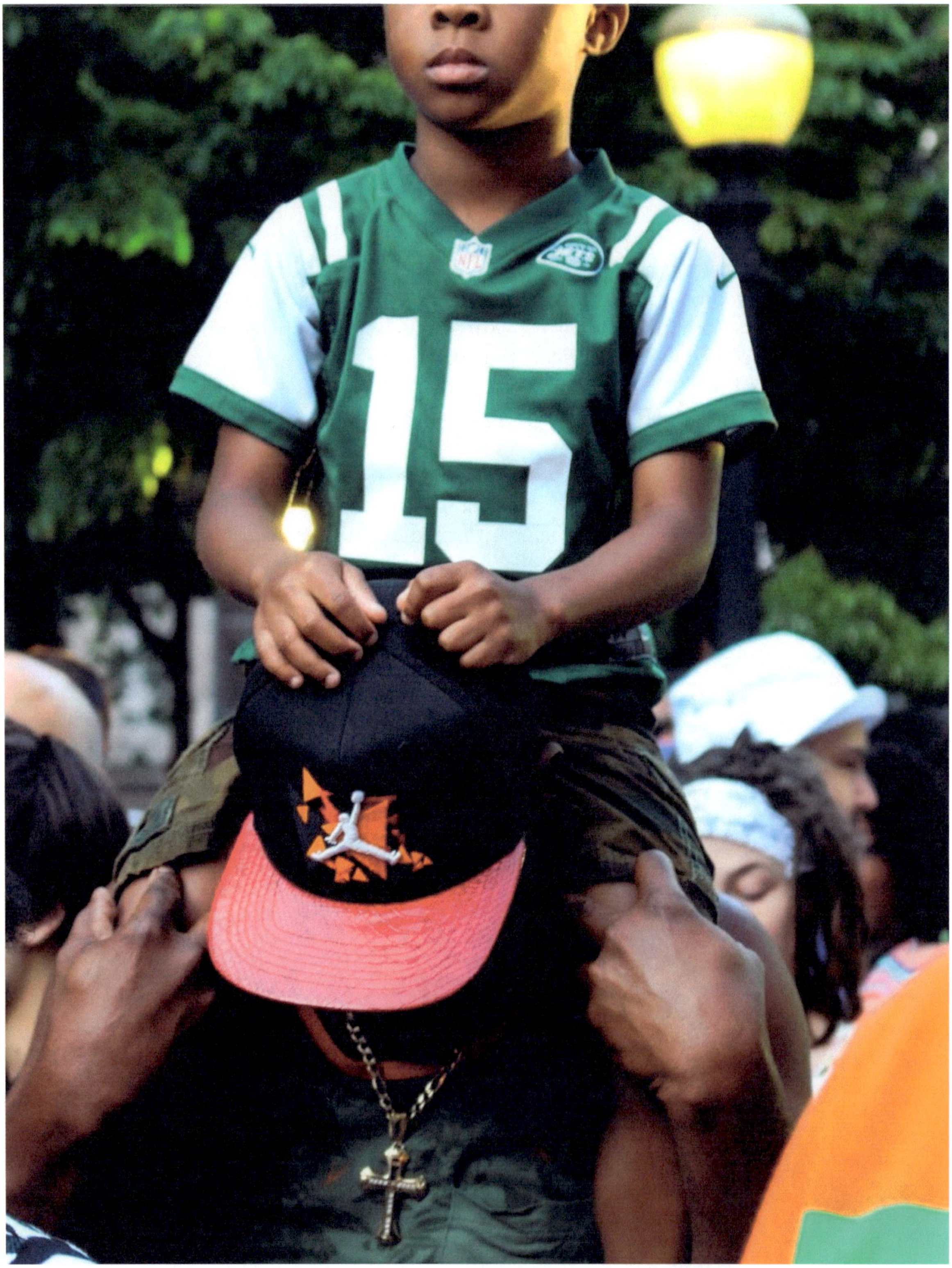
15

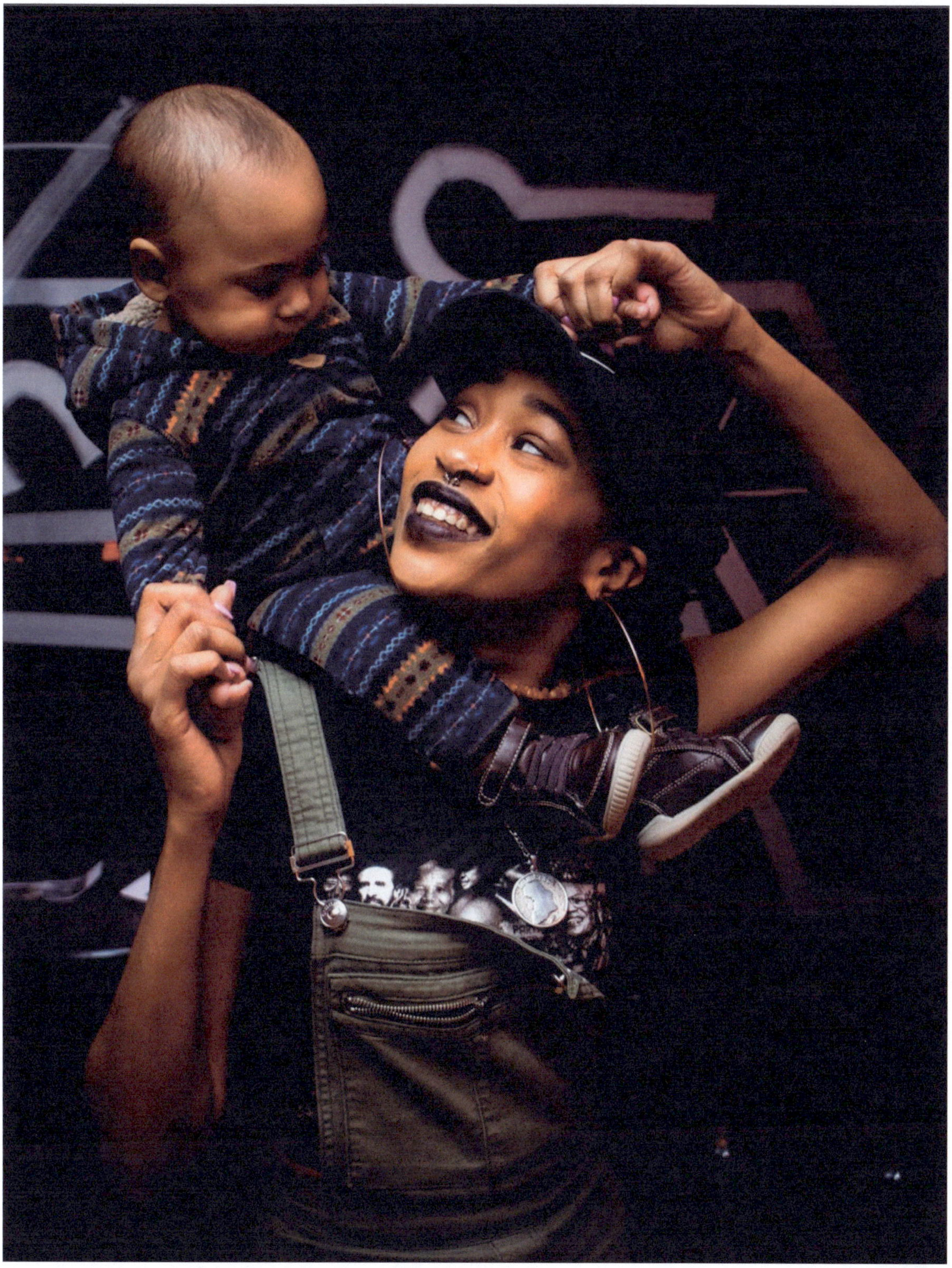

WASH YOUR BACK

You've texted me stressed out from another day of work

For a moment I feel like less of a man because, in this moment I'm incapable of helping you find a solution to your problems

After which I have to pep talk myself and remember that I need to step outside of my ego

And that you called me because, maybe not always, but sometimes I understand you better than your journal does

And that is all you ask for

So, after I've given myself time to digest and regroup, I text back and reassure you that I love you

and that, if it's not too much I have 2 requests of you

Already having so much on your plate you reluctantly ask what they are

Request #1

When you sign off for the day, can you promise me that whatever frustrations and problems you have there, you'll try your best not to bring home with you?

And when you get home, I'll tell you what my next request is.

Hours later, you come home to a clean apartment and dinner already served while the dishes are being cleaned

Still anxious from what my next request may be, you ignore all of this and go straight to the bedroom to find the shower running and call me to the room to ask why

I kiss you on your forehead and say, well that's request #2

Let me wash your back

The hard-to-reach parts that you usually contort yourself to cleanse

The back that you allow your boss' racist remarks roll off of

The back that hides the knots created by decades of trauma that you're still healing from

Let me wash it
Let me watch the soap run down your spine and lead me to every scar and tattoo

The tattoo at the nape of your neck that not only reminds you that you're an Empress but reminds ME that if I treat you anything less than that, your back will be the last thing I see

All the way down to the scar that still houses the metal shards from an IED that you survived while fighting for this country's rights to take yours away from you

If you don't mind, please hand me your exfoliating gloves

Let me scrub the back that your exes have used as a stepping stone to make themselves better men for the women they're with today

The back that stood against the wall while the man that told he loved you, used you as his punching bag, leaving you to not only fight for your life but the life that you didn't know you were carrying in your belly

Now my name isn't Jesus and I don't have a God complex but PLEASE…

Please let me wash these burdens away

Because I get it

And from this point forward, I got your back

And I know there will be days I need you too

That's why I'm gonna lean up against you, you just lean right back against me. This way, we don't have to sleep with our heads in the mud.

So babe, Can I wash your back?

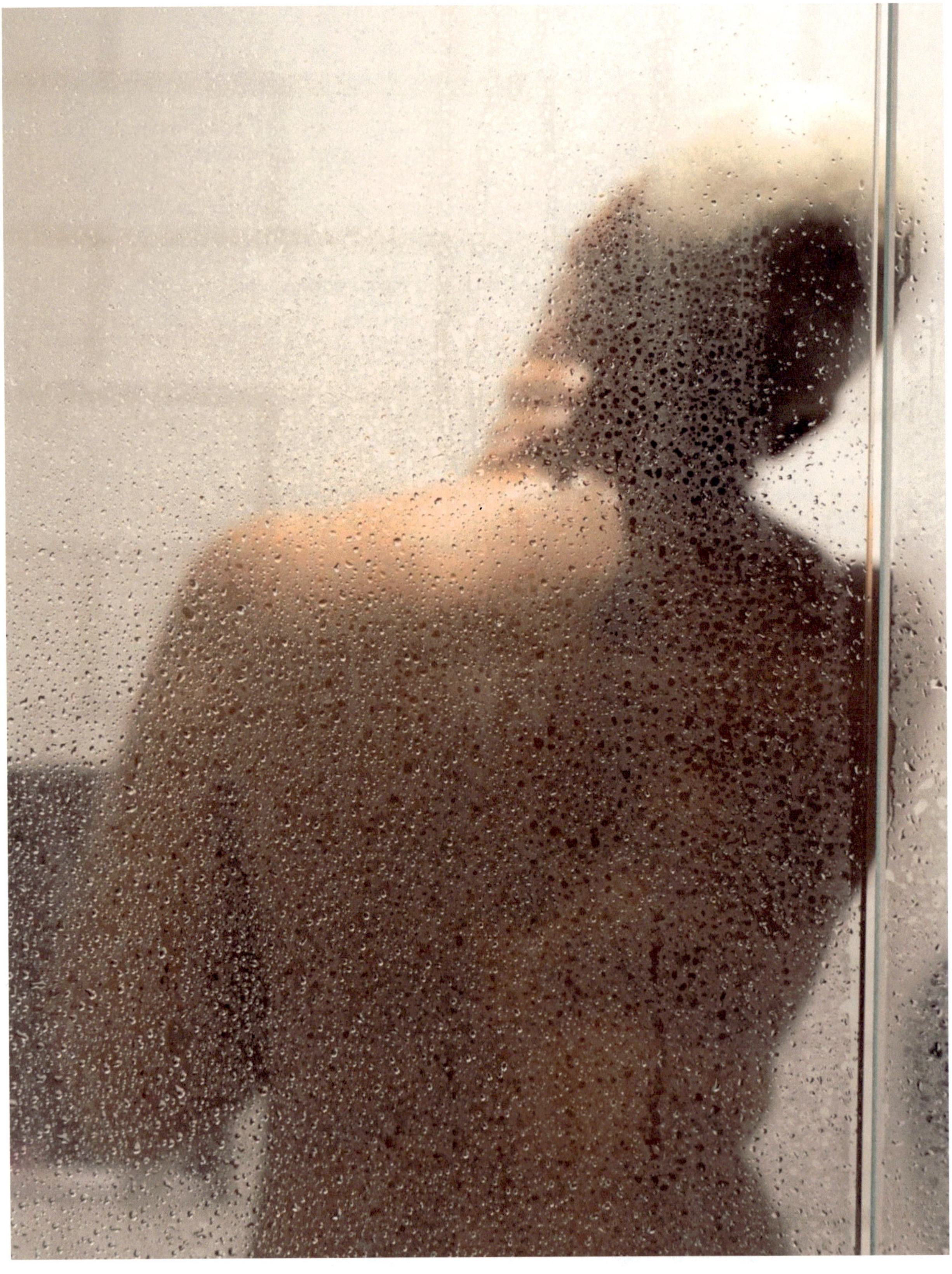

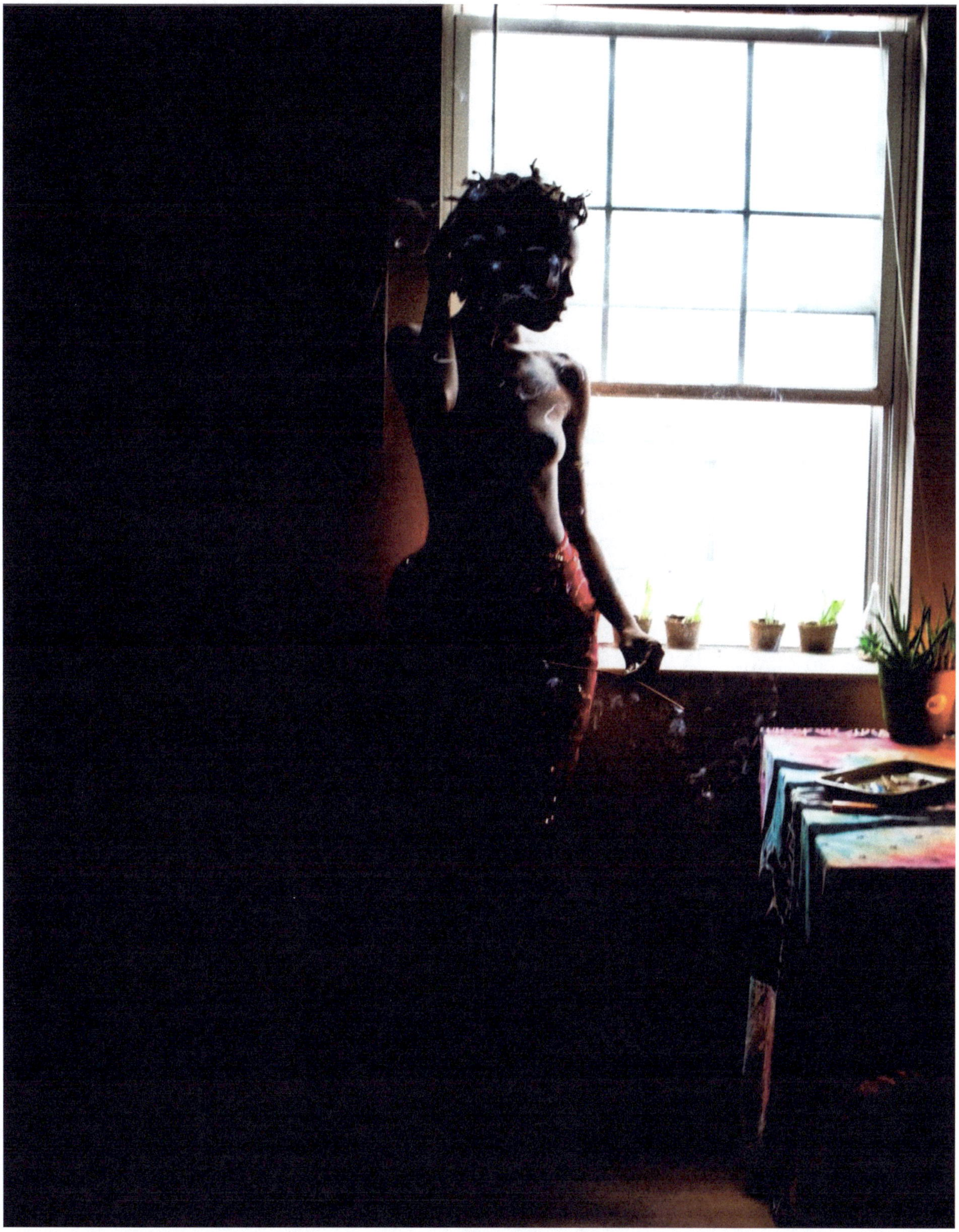

DIVORCING MY MUSE

Dear Muse,

I write this letter with teary eyes because for so long you were all I knew. The first thought of every morning and the last thought at night. We were once inseparable. 2 peas in a pod and though we never put a title on it, for so long you were my best friend. As so many others have come and gone there were times you were all I had. I have so many vague memories of nights where you'd lull me to sleep as I bathed in tears and liquor and like the loyal one that you are, you'd be right there to wake me up the next morning. I loved you. In fact, I loved you so much that you were the common topic of every poem, song and short story I ever wrote. And the better I became; I've always given you credit for helping me reach a higher level. Because, in my eyes, without you I was nothing. My love for you was so strong that whether I wanted to or not, I took you everywhere with me. Even in those short periods when we took breaks from one another l, you'd always find your way into my new relationships. Staying so close that each relationship became involuntarily polyamorous. But you required so much attention that they would always leave because you just had to make sure everyone knew who really ran the show. I could leave because before I knew it, I'd become co-dependent. With you so long that we'd become a common law marriage. But I didn't care because I felt like you made me great. Each verse, each stanza, each photo more potent than the last because they were all influenced by you. I had stopped being happy in this relationship long ago because I didn't know who I would be without you. But I've finally decided that it's time to find out.

So, when you read this, consider yourself served because Pain, I'm divorcing you! I've met someone better. Only through healing have I been able to stop seeing the world through blood-stained glasses and find her. Someone that has soothed the anxiety that happiness once used to cause me because I knew it wouldn't last. Someone who has grabbed me by the hand and patiently walked me through the other side of chaos to show me what life looks like in the light
Someone that has showed me that the grass is greener in a world where I don't need an Instagram filter. Someone who has shown me what love is supposed to feel like and for her I have truly fallen
Her name? Her name is Peace.
And in order for me to hold on to her, I must sever ties with you
I know you're everywhere. So, bumping into you is inevitable but just know I'll keep every conversation short and sweet. Because since I've found Peace, she's the only thing I choose to entertain. I don't know who I'll be without her or even if I'll still be able to write another poem but she's worth the risk. So, to you, Pain, I wish you goodbye.
I'll leave my ring and my keys by the door
As for everything I've gained since being with you, you can have it.
I no longer desire any of it
What I have now is so much better that I begin and end every encounter with her name
And for your sake, I hope you find your own version of what I have…
PEACE

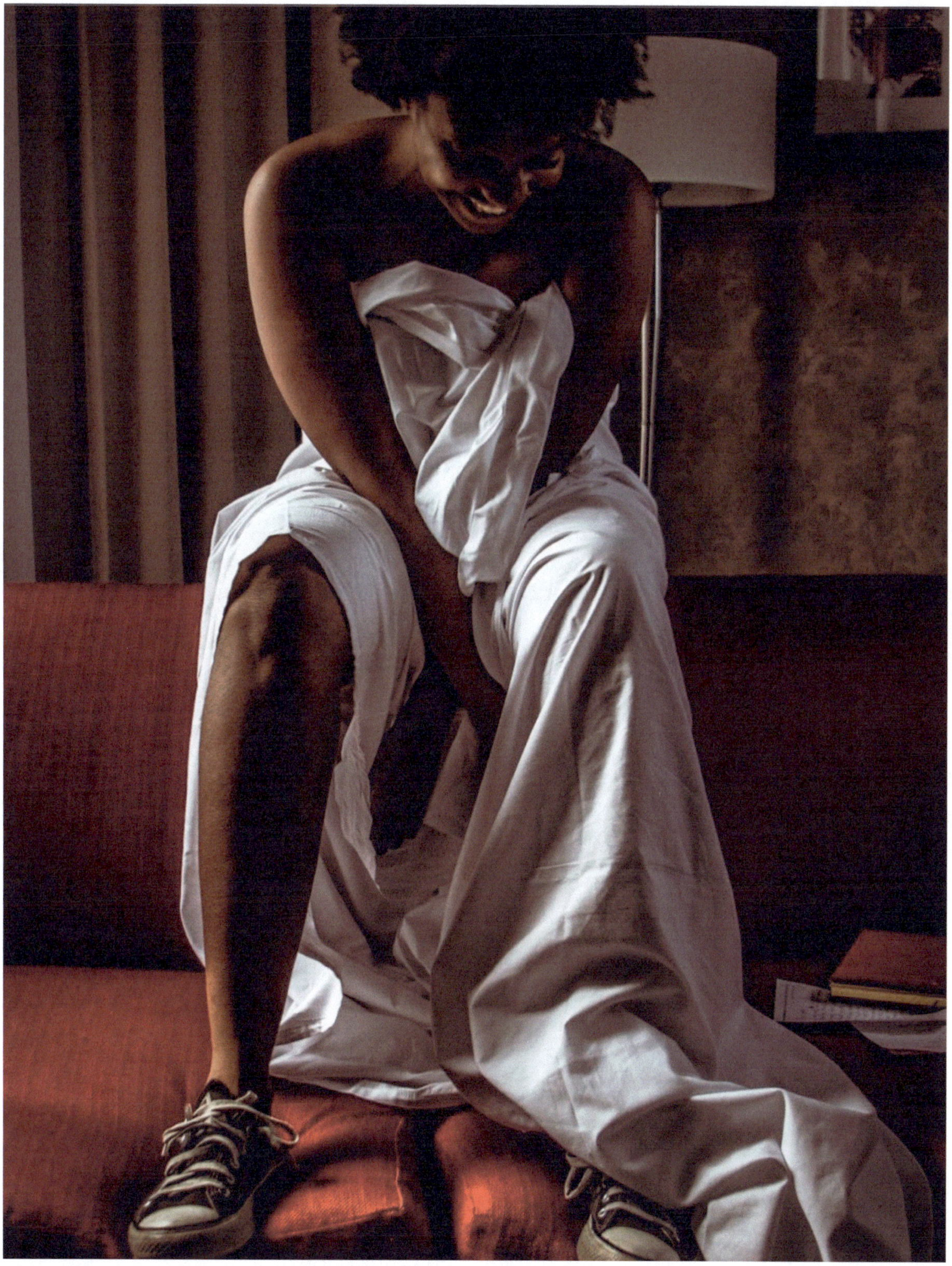

...for Love

"I bet you wonder where I've been..."

Alone.

Drifting away at sea without a GPS hoping to find myself eventually on an island known as romance

But I've lost the wind in my sails and I had so much faith that I knew where I was going in the past that I threw my oars overboard years ago

Now as I look out at the horizon with no destination in sight it would appear that I've become the salty one

"...I search to find a love within"

But I'm a Leo, so if astrology is accurate

Then self-love is hardly a concept that I struggle with

It's no wonder I hit repeat when Jhene Aiko said, "I love me enough for the both of us."

"You see I wrote this to let you know

That I'm in love with love and I can't let go"

I'm perfectly comfortable with being alone

And if we're being honest, being single seems a lot more peaceful and convenient

So, if you're confused then I can relate because I confuse myself too

Which is why

"MY FRIENDS WONDER WHAT IS WRONG WITH ME. BUT IM IN A DAZE, LOOKING FOR LOVE, YOU SEE"

Because ultimately, I know that no one lives forever

And I want to know what it feels like to be loved correctly while I'm alive

At least in the romantic sense

Because I seem to have devolved from hopeless romantic to romantically hopeless

And addict chasing that 1st high until he eventually overdoses

"Some people go around the world for love but they will never find what they dream of"

I've tried flares, Morse code and even smoke signals

Yet here I am… feeling blue and left on read

I was always taught that true love is a braid composed of 2 souls and their God

Yet I continue Drifting.

Double-stranded

"What you won't do for love. You've tried everything. Don't give up.

WHAT ARE YOU LOOKING FOR?

What Are You Looking For?

If you're currently single and actively dating right now then I can guarantee you've been asked the same boring interview question

"What are you looking for?"

To put it plain, I want a best friend

But where I always failed in the past is confusing platonic love for romantic

Misreading cues because my opposite sex friends often treated me better than the women I chose to date

But I guess when you're used to fast food, even a McRib tastes like Ruth's Chris

So if we're sticking to that metaphor, you're going to eat whatever's served to you until you realize that you deserve to take the time to sit back and refine your palate

I want to move beyond the surface

I'm nearly 40 and don't have the mental capacity to memorize another favorite color or pretend I know the personality traits assigned to your zodiac sign

Allow me to get to know you by showing me your favorite films or books

Give me the chance to get to know you intimately through the art you both consume and create

So I can understand what molded what may be one of the greatest pieces of art only few will be privileged to see,

your soul.

Teach me your love languages so I can learn how to speak them fluently

because I know what it's like to be with someone that never cared to try.

FYI, mine is quality time and I love to learn new things so every hour spent getting to know you gives me another moment to fall in love with the subject

And can't afford to miss a class.

Teach me what comforts you so I know how to help you find peace after a stressful day

I need to know if I need to have a bubble bath drawn or a blunt rolled

Do I need to learn to cook your favorite meal or are we calling for delivery?

Or maybe you prefer some Miles Davis and a good book

I need to learn how to be your peace because I also expect you to be mine

I've never had a problem with date nights or hanging with friends

But I want someone who also sees the beauty in being able to be alone, together.

That comma was very important.

Because I love my alone time but I also want your presence in the process

But you also gotta understand that I'm not the type to fill every moment of silence with conversation

Just BE with me and let our souls do the talking

I'd also prefer to date a creative

Like Phenix said, I'd like to marry an artist because I need someone to know that if I disappear for a few hours, it's not cuz I'm creepin. It's because I'm creating

Someone who understands that my camera isn't bait I use to meet women

Cuz I'd like to think I do that well enough on my own

Beauty is good but I'd prefer to love a woman from the inside-out.

Beauty fades but when nurtured correctly, the soul remains the same

And I'd prefer your heart over the ones that appear on my screen when I double-tap

Nor do I mind ceasing engagement WITH them as long as it means being engaged TO you

A few seconds of dopamine doesn't equate to a lifetime wearing your ring

My best friend

My peace

My muse

My forever

This is what I desire

Is that you?

Inquire Within.

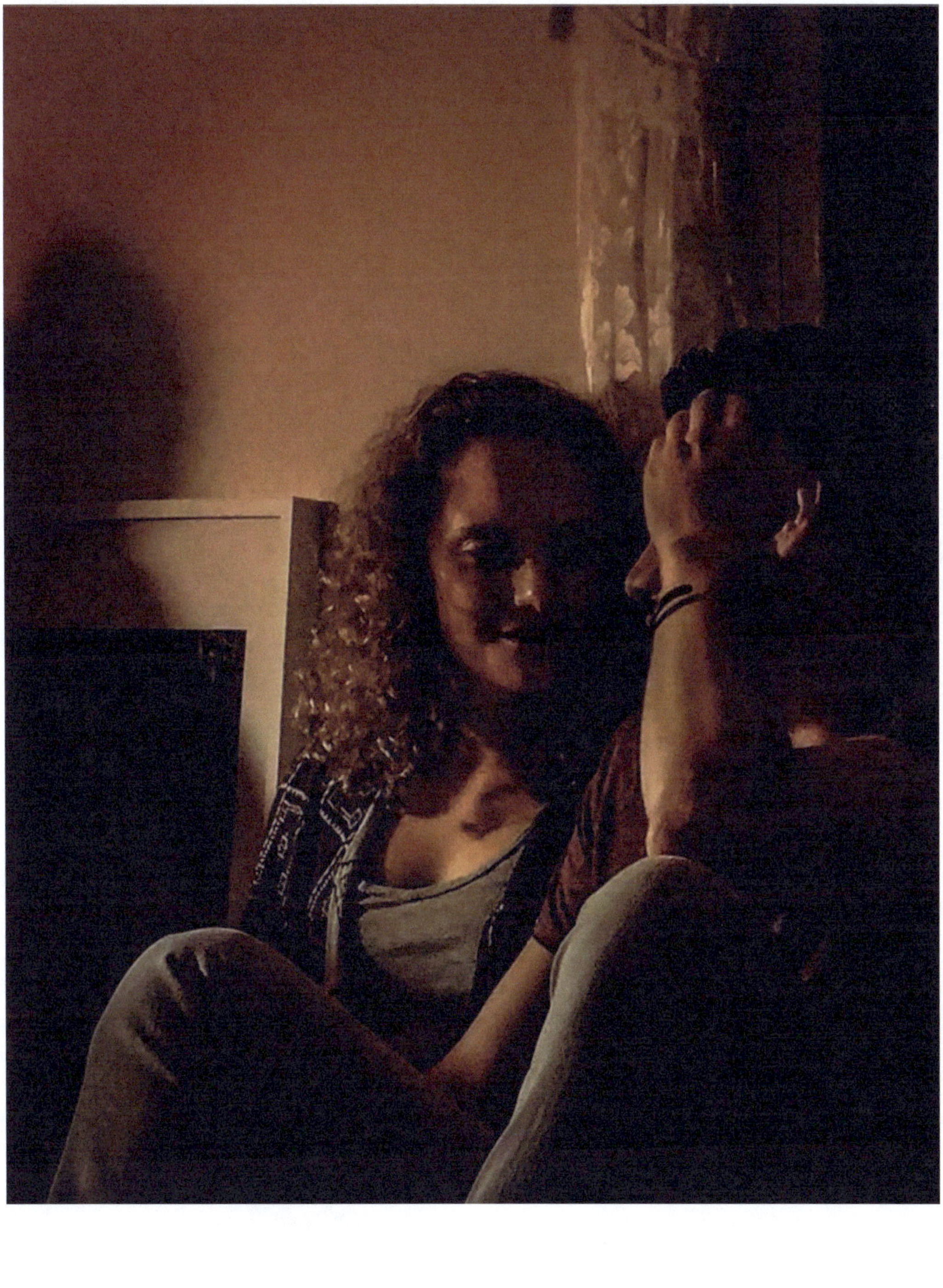

PROSE

Once we were introduced it didn't take long for me to fall in love with you. I became mesmerized as letters became words, words became sentences, sentences into paragraphs and formed a letter; this letter. A love letter to you, Prose. It is you that makes sense out of nonsense, abstract figures and foreign characters and turns those characters into friends.

My favorite subject; fitting that I prose on about you to any that will listen. Much like your name, you seem "scattered" to the short-sighted but you make perfect sense to those patient enough to allow the bigger picture that your words so vividly paint reveal the truth. With love and gratitude, I thank you.

Creatively Yours,

RaShaun "T.B." Letif

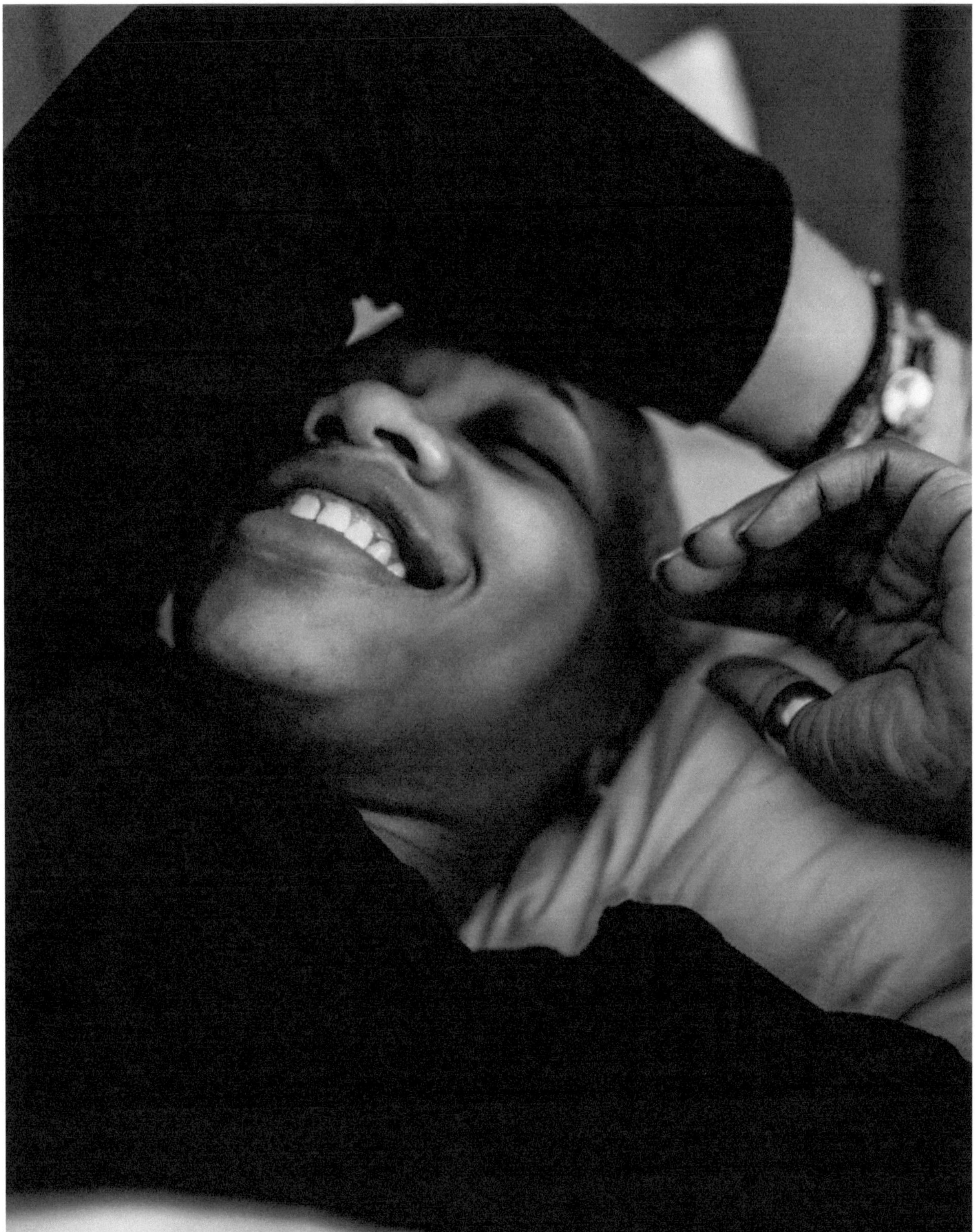

DEBT TO SOBRIETY

This story starts when I was 7

The baby of 10 but I had my own slice of heaven

My only problem was my Ninja Turtles needed weapons

Pay attention all'a that's about change up in a second

A typical Friday night

Mom n pops tired

Just another weekend on the east end

Nobody flinched when we heard the shots fired

Less than an hour later police knocked on the door

Not allowing them to finish their statement

My father pushed passed them and ran out in his draws

I was too young to realize they came by to for my brother's body to be identified

1990, July 29th... the 1st time I saw a grown man cry

This is the 1st memory I have of my childhood

Before that everything else is a haze

Yusef Jamal Belcher left for dead in the street at 17 years of age

You live by the street you die by the street, there's nothin anyone could've done

But soon after, my father would turn to drugs to cope with the pain of losing a son

Now remember I was a child when Jamal's life was took

Far too young to realize that my father was strung out on the same substance my brother pushed

Fast forward a few years when I'm in my adolescence

All my brothers have moved out now I'm the man of the house and I'm disgusted by his presence

The man that once taught me the ten-step program left to take 12 of his own

imagine my surprise when I put on a pair of his pants and I reach in to find a pocket full of stones

This must have been his sobering moment cuz he gave his life to God to see brighter days

But he promised me he was done once before so I'm still lookin at him sideways

He finally turned his life around and was committed to keeping it right

Then cancer crept in to take his life like a thief in the night

You once told me "The day God feels you can't handle what he gives you is the day he doesn't wake you

Labor Day weekend 2012 was when he decided to take you

Sometimes I wonder why u ain't standing here beside me

I guess you paid your debt to sobriety

Now picture a teenage boy fluent in street talk and passive aggression

Only 18 years of age turning to liquor to battle his depression

I open up to my boys just tryna get em to understand

They said stop bein a pussy and go get you some pussy; it's time to grow up nigga, be a man

18 years old I grew a dependency to liquor and casual sexing

Somehow thinking I was better than my father because I had different vices to cope with my depression

From the bottom of a bottle to the bottom of her box

I'm in a perpetual state of hate and the cycle doesn't stop

Till one night I realize there's no amount of liquor to quiet the voices that I'm hearing

I lost all control of my actions and the next morning I woke up to realize why they call it spirits

I just want this shit to end and there's only one way out

My roommate walked in just in time to snatch that bottle of bleach from my mouth

Please don't call me RaShaun no more, call me Letif

RaShaun died on the night that I tried to drink that bleach

Somethings gotta give cuz I ain't doin well

I quit my job, hit the reset button and moved to ATL

By 2014 I moved back and had a child with my best friend

Born 3 months early and didn't make it thru the night

Yale Hospital is where we left him

So, dad I wrote this piece to say I'm sorry I grew to resent you

Cuz god made me hold my son while he took his last breath to understand what you went thru

As if burying my child wasn't enough this is where it hurts

One long look in the mirror made me realize I was repeating your cycle but in reverse

A carousel of bad decisions that went round and round like karma

Some people are products of their environment but I'm a product of my trauma

And you wonder why I show you this side of me?

I guess this is my debt to sobriety

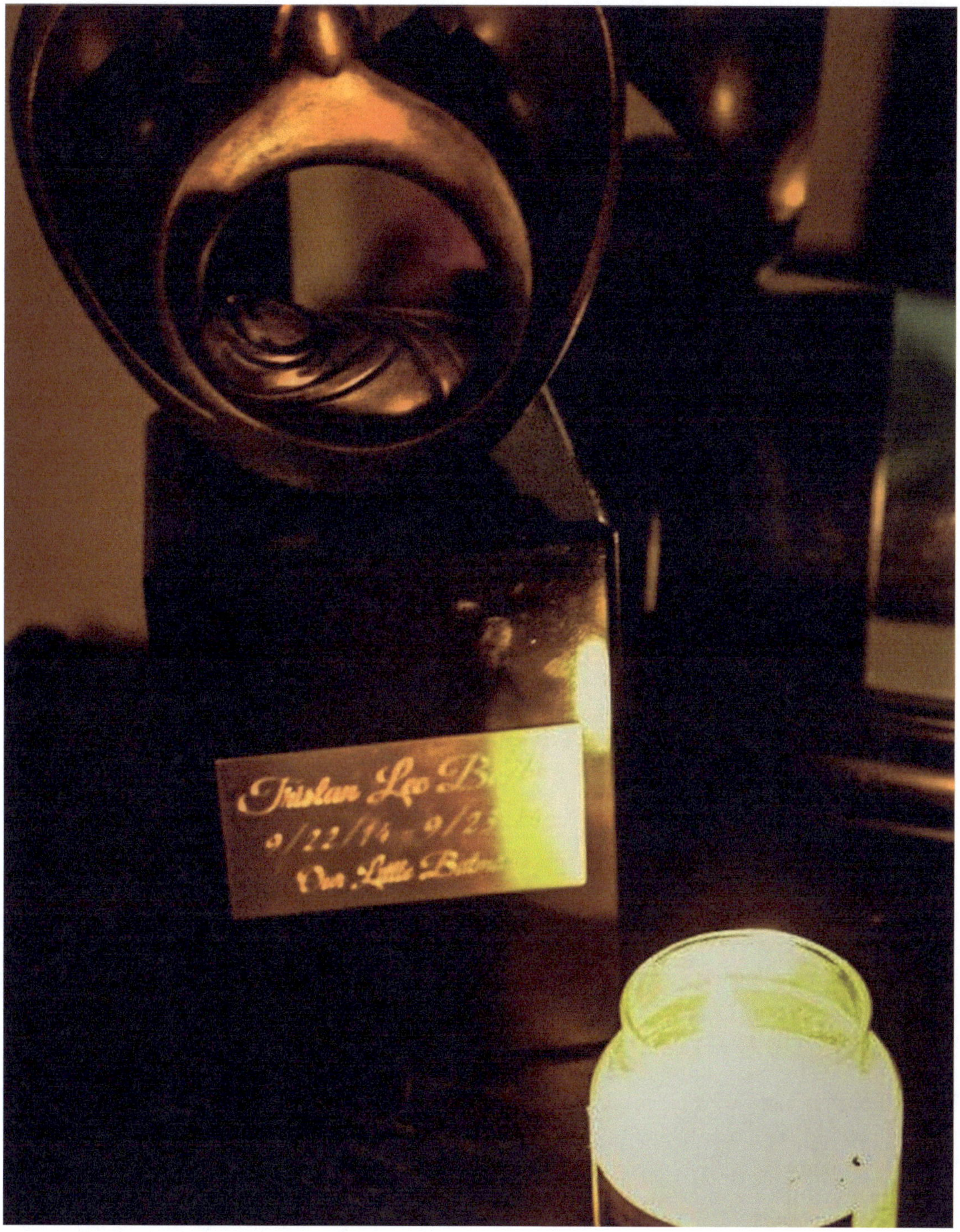

WHEN I'M GONE

Do you ever think about life after death;

Not only in the spiritual sense but also how your loved ones will be affected by your absence?

I tell my family and friends I love them as often as I can because I know that it may be the last thing I get to say to them

It makes some uncomfortable. I think maybe because they feel obligated to say it back when in actuality, I just want someone's least memory of me to be a good one

And tell my love that the reason I say "Thank you" when she tells me she loves me is because I see God when I look into her eyes so sometimes it wasn't actually HER I was talking to

When I'm gone, I pray it doesn't weigh too heavily on those with whom I've had petty "beef" with and those that chose distance over accountability

Let it be known that you've been forgiven and regardless of how much you've said "Fuck Letif" I've continued rooting for you.

When I'm gone don't be sad, cuz I'll be heading straight to my family reunion!

A bittersweet event where I hope to receive forgiveness for my emotional detachment and get the opportunity to ask all the questions about our family ancestry that I didn't get to ask in the physical realm

Don't be sad because I'll get to know my brother a little more and hear my sister's laugh again. I'll get to smoke one with my uncle and share another laugh my grandmother. I'll finally meet my father's parents and ask them what it was like raising 3 Black boys in the civil rights era. I'll get to talk to my father about everything my mom has been up to while finally getting the chance to play with my son.

If I'm lucky enough to be married, I'll do my best in life to make sure she knows that she'll still be loved in eternity. Because while the vows say "Until death do you part" there was no part that said I had to stop loving you. I'll be waiting for her in the afterlife and apply for a job to be a guardian angel for her and our kids.

When I'm Gone, bury me in a Black-on-Black suit with a tuxedo lapel cuz if this is the last thing I'm going to be wearing, I need to be red carpet fresh when my loved ones see my spirit watching over them at night. And don't forget to bury me with my glasses because Vada taught me that even in the afterlife, I can't see without them.

When I'm gone, you got 48 hours to get all the crying out and then I want y'all to plan the party! Because after you mourn my death, I need you to celebrate my life! Pass around cigars and drink bourbon until the only tears come from laughter from telling all the embarrassing stories of the dumb things I did while alive.

I don't know how they'd pull it off but I want a DJ to play a set that consisted of joints by Anita Baker, Brandy, WuTang, The Roots, Kendrick, Kelis and Kaytranada because if I'm gonna do one thing, it's remind people that my favorites may not have sold billions of records but they're still better than theirs.

Hang the photos of my loved ones on the walls of the repast so maybe then they see that each image was a monument to how much I loved them. May the only photos of me in my obituary be the ones from my social media feed. By me posting them, you can pretty much consider those preapproved. And please do not put those weird clouds behind me or put those tacky wings on my back. I was far from an angel while I lived and while I'd like to believe I'm going upstairs, there's no guarantee what destination will be written on my boarding pass.

When I'm gone, put this piece somewhere for safe keeping because if you're reading this it means you loved me enough to keep a part of me with you and as long as it's in your possession, a part of me will live on forever.

Thank you.

IN LOVING MEMORY

I HOPE I'M MAKING
YOU PROUD

BRAD BELCHER

KATHERINE JACKSON

WAYMON "WAY-WAY" BELCHER

MONIQUE BELCHER

TRISTAN BELCHER

YUSEF JAMAL BELCHER
(NOT PHOTOGRAPHED BY BELCHER DIGITAL)

ABOUT THE AUTHOR

RaShaun "Prince" Letif Belcher was always a creative. From drawing at a young age and making up short stories about the characters he'd create, to writing poetry to express feelings that he didn't think he had anyone to express them with. He also took dance class in middle school and continued dancing until falling in love with photography in high school. It was his high school photography teacher that inspired him to bring his camera with him everywhere he went. There are countless pictures of his loved ones and many more to come. Always one to wear his heart on this sleeve, he's grateful for the ability to allow others to see the world through his lens; both with his words and his camera.

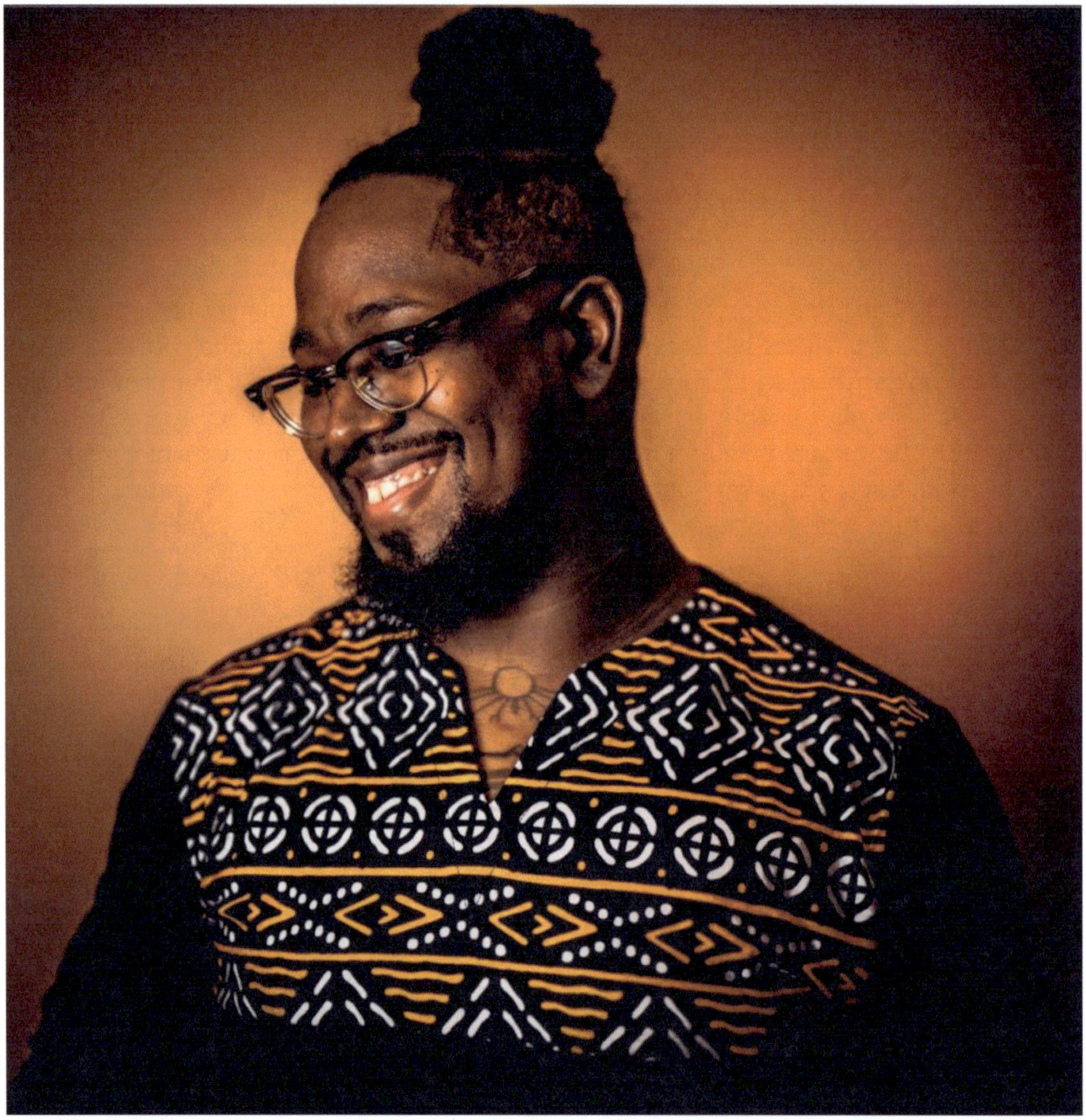

Special Thanks & Acknowledgements

I would just like to thank my family for the love and support I've been privileged to enjoy throughout the course of my life. My parents, Brad and Toni. My siblings Che, Eliot, Monique, Kenyatta, Bebe, Tameeka, Jamon, Jamal and Shayla. My nieces and nephews Aisha, Zoe, Bailey, Ej, Maya, Brandon, Shakila, Shakeem, Imani, Najee, Jaaziel, Imara, Sharash, Dayanah, and Eric III. Uncle Marty & Aunt Shirley, Uncle Way-Way, Uncle Darrel & Aunt Debbie F, Uncle Demus and Aunt Debbie H. All the hundreds of cousins lol.

My "Day 1's", Shawn, Sleep, Eric, Kevin E, James, Raul & Courtney.

My Godchildren: Ari, Ayanna and Pharoahe

My creative family; Duck, Ernel, Natalie, Jerome, Phenix, D- Dubb, Denzel, Syrin, Nate Gxfted, Ajani, B Wilds, Influence, Nikki, Rahz, TruePoetry, Tymani, Musa, Serenity, Jazz E, Jessica V, Erma, Charity, Aleecya, Greg, TeeKay, Big Rich, SMillz, Juice Jonz, Krystal, Jules, Zulie, Alicia, Gaby, Professor Lex, Big Rich, Roachfat, Silent Quill, Red Flag, Char, Shanice, Jedi, Zeze, Nell, Shay and Amber.

Pachet, I thank you for the wealth of knowledge you shared with me and the abundance of love you gave. Thank you for believing in me and pushing me to be better than I was the day before. It's a shame things happened the way they did but the love will always be there.

Lady Obsidian Rain, my Partner-in-Crime! We sat side by side many times working on our books together and now we're both done! I'm proud of you and thank you for always trying to bring me back from those dark places.

To the mother of my Son, Melo, thank you for being one of the best friends I ever had and thank you for giving me one of the best gifts I could ever receive in our son Tristan. Love you always.

Mom, had to come back to you again. Thank you for raising me and teaching me to be the man I am today and for being the lighthouse every time I found myself lost at sea. I love you most!

To the friendships and relationships that died up to this point, know that I thank you for the good times and that I love you.

Made in the USA
Columbia, SC
25 January 2025